IT'S ALL ABOUT THE PROMPTS!

THE BUSINESS AI PLAYBOOK:

A GUIDE OF **POWERFUL AI** PROMPTS FOR ANY BUSINESS TO USE IN 2023/24.

Its All About The Prompts

Volume 1, Volume 1

Stephen Finnegan

Published by Stephen Finnegan, 2023.

While every precaution has been taken in the preparation of this book, the publisher assumes no responsibility for errors or omissions, or for damages resulting from the use of the information contained herein.

ITS ALL ABOUT THE PROMPTS

First edition. September 20, 2023.

ISBN: 979-8223113782

Written by Stephen Finnegan.

The Business AI Playbook: A Guide to Powerful AI Prompts for Any Business to Use in 2023/24.

The Business AI Playbook: A Guide to Powerful AI Prompts for Any Business to Use in 2023/24.

Introduction

In the age of digitisation, business landscapes have experienced a profound transformation, powered not just by the sheer force of technology, but by the intricate dance of interaction between machines and human intentions.

Central to this ballet is the rise of Artificial Intelligence (AI), which is already to revolutionise how businesses operate, compete, and innovate. It also will affect how consumers also seek information about products and services.

Yet, as with any sophisticated tool, the true efficacy of AI lies not just in its computational prowess but in the finesse with which it's directed.

Enter **AI prompts**: the subtle, yet potent, instructions that guide AI models to generate relevant insights, responses, or actions from a human user.

Using the correct AI prompts is analogous to asking the right questions in a strategic business meeting. They determine the direction, depth, and relevance of the outcomes.

When finely tuned, these prompts can enable businesses to extract actionable insights from vast datasets, enhance customer experiences, streamline operations, and even foster innovation in products and services.

"Conversely, vague, or improperly phrased prompts can result in misguided answers, wasted time and resources, and missed opportunities."

In the subsequent sections, we'll delve deeper into the nuances of constructing effective AI prompts and explore how businesses across sectors are leveraging this power to drive efficiency, growth, and sustainable advantage in an increasingly complex local and international market sectors.

As we embark on this journey, one thing becomes clear: in the AI-driven world of business, it's not just about having the right tools, but about mastering the art of communication with them.

Also, I have included at the end of this eBook, a list of **275+ AI Business Related Prompts** to test and evaluate for your business departments.

To get started, let's dive in with the best prompt ideas that will assist you and your business going forward.

Familiarise yourself with the capabilities and limitations of artificial intelligence.

Beware - AI is – Not a **Magic Solution** to solving All Business Problems.

However, the technology has solid potential to assist and help transform

your business organisation.

Improved and **New AI Systems** will no doubt become
available as time goes by ...

Chapter 1: Key Business AI Prompts to Get Started in 2023/24:

You can type any prompt into an AI system, and it will reply, however for using AI in business, you need to know what **power prompts** can provide you with the best results giving the edge over the competition.

In later chapters you will learn about using AI in business along with useful recommendations and advice.

What Exactly is an AI Prompt - An AI prompt is a specific input or instruction given to an artificial intelligence system, often in the form of a text-based query or command, to elicit a specific response or output.

In the context of models like OpenAI's GPT series, a prompt can be a question, a statement, or any form of text that guides the AI in generating relevant and coherent text in return.

For instance:

If you give the AI model a prompt like "Describe the process of photosynthesis," the AI will return a description or explanation about photosynthesis.

If you ask, "Write a short story about a robot," the model will generate a short story on the given topic.

Prompts act as triggers or cues to guide the model's response, making them essential for shaping the direction and nature of AI-generated content. In a way, they define the context or frame the type of information you're seeking from the AI.

Below is a curated AI Prompt list for Business Users, to test and use across several main business departments and categories.

How 'UpToDate' is AI Data?

Always check how 'UpToDate' any AI platform training data is. For example, **Chat GPT's** training data at the time of writing this eBook (Sep 2023) is only based on data as of September 2021.

Bard AI (Google) for example - Bard's data is constantly being updated with new information. The data trained on includes text from books, articles, websites, and other sources. This data is updated on a regular basis, so Bard AI is always learning new things faster than other AI systems.

However, it is important to remember that **Bard AI** is still under development, and the data is not always up to date. If you are looking for information on a specific topic, it is always best to check multiple sources.

Other AI systems, and there are many, also have training date up to a certain date, so check regularly how updated each AI systems information is.

A company called 'ClickUp' keeps a record of all AI systems, you can visit

their listings page - bit.ly/44JG495[1]

Key Business AI Prompting by Departments:

Let's dive in and review useful prompts to use by department. All Prompts are dependent on what business information you make available to an AI system for analysis or review.

1. Market Analysis:

- Predict market trends for the next quarter.
- Identify potential competitors in our niche.
- Analyse customer sentiment towards our brand.
- Extract the most common features mentioned in product reviews.
- Highlight emerging industries for potential investment.

2. Competitor Analysis:

1. Overview and Market Presence

- Generate a summary of each competitor's company history, mission, and vision.
- Highlight key products/services offered by each competitor.
- Estimate the market share of each competitor.

1. Product/Service Analysis

---

1. https://dev-share.clickup.com/9805000210/gr/h/946rvgj-16/

6be1ba8fcf3f101?_gl=1*6rfysz*_gcl_au*MTcxNDczMzI2Ny4xNjkzODQyMjcy

- Compare the features and benefits of our product/ service with those of competitors.
- Analyse user reviews and sentiment towards each competitor's offerings.
- Determine the unique selling propositions (USPs) of each competitor.

1. **Pricing Strategy**

- Evaluate the pricing models adopted by competitors.
- Identify any discounting or promotional strategies in play.
- Compare the perceived value proposition against the price point for each competitor.

1. **Technology and Innovation**

- Analyse the technology stack used by competitors.
- Determine if competitors have made significant investments in AI, ML, or other emerging technologies.
- Highlight any patents, proprietary technologies, or innovations brought by competitors to the market.

1. **Marketing and Brand Presence**

- Evaluate competitors' online presence (website, social media channels, etc.).
- Analyse the content and messaging strategies of competitors.
- Examine any influencer partnerships, endorsements,

or major ad campaigns run by competitors.

1. **Sales Channels and Distribution**

- Identify the primary and secondary sales channels used by competitors.
- Determine if competitors have any exclusive distribution deals or partnerships.
- Examine the geographic regions/markets where competitors have a strong presence.

1. **Customer Base and Loyalty**
    - Analyse customer segments targeted by competitors.
    - Examine customer feedback, testimonials, and loyalty programs of competitors.
    - Identify any potential gaps in the market that competitors are not addressing.
2. **Operational Efficiency**
    - Evaluate the supply chain and operations model of competitors.
    - Determine if competitors have adopted any automation or optimized processes to cut costs.
    - Highlight any sustainability or environmental initiatives undertaken by competitors.
3. **Financial Performance**
    - Analyse the annual revenue, profitability, and growth rate of competitors.

- ○ Compare key financial ratios and performance metrics among competitors.
- ○ Highlight any major investments, mergers, or acquisitions made by competitors recently.

4. **SWOT Analysis**
   - ○ Use AI to generate a SWOT (Strengths, Weaknesses, Opportunities, Threats) analysis for each competitor.
   - ○ Highlight areas where our company has a competitive advantage.
   - ○ Identify potential threats and opportunities based on competitor activities.

1. **Future Predictions**
   - ○ Predict the future moves or strategies competitors might adopt based on historical data and current trends.
   - ○ Identify industries or markets where competitors might expand.

2. **Cultural and Ethical Analysis**
   - ○ Assess competitors' company culture, values, and ethical stances.
   - ○ Highlight any major controversies or reputational challenges faced by competitors.

2. Financial Forecasting:

- Predict next month's sales based on current data.

- Forecast quarterly expenses.
- Calculate ROI for our recent marketing campaign.
- Analyse discrepancies in our accounting.
- Compare our financial growth rate against competitors.

3. Operations & Logistics:

- Optimise supply chain routes.
- Forecast inventory needs for the next six months.
- Identify potential bottlenecks in our production process.
- Suggest improvements for warehousing efficiency.
- Predict maintenance schedules for machinery.

4. HR & Talent Management:

- Screen resumes for the most suitable candidates for a role.
- Analyse employee satisfaction from feedback forms.
- Predict which departments might face staffing shortages.
- Suggest training programs for upskilling employees.
- Identify patterns in employee turnover.

5. Customer Insights & CRM:

- Segment our customer base for targeted marketing.
- Predict which customers might churn next month.
- Recommend products/services to specific customer segments.

- Analyse the effectiveness of our customer support.
- Extract common queries from customer emails.

6. Marketing & Branding:

- A/B test email campaign headlines.
- Predict the performance of our next social media campaign.
- Generate content ideas for our blog.
- Analyse the performance of our competitors' ads.
- Recommend influencers in our industry to collaborate with.

7. Product Development & Innovation:

- Extract features customers desire from feedback.
- Predict the success of a new product launch.
- Recommend areas of innovation in our product lineup.
- Generate product names based on certain criteria.
- Evaluate the feasibility of proposed product changes.

8. Sales & Lead Generation:

- Recommend businesses to partner with for mutual growth.
- Predict the success rate of various sales pitches.
- Identify trends in sales data.
- Generate script ideas for cold outreach.
- Recommend events or conferences to attend for lead generation.

9. IT & Cybersecurity:

- Monitor network for unusual activities.
- Recommend updates to our current cybersecurity measures.
- Predict potential IT outages.
- Suggest optimizations for our website's UX.
- Analyse the speed and performance of our online platforms.

10. Strategic Planning & Decision Making:

- Extract key points from a business proposal.
- Predict the impact of global events on our operations.
- Recommend areas of expansion or contraction.
- Generate a list of business opportunities in a specific market.
- Evaluate the long-term sustainability of our current business model.

11. Customer Service & Support:

- Recommend solutions to common customer issues.
- Analyse response times and efficiency of support teams.
- Predict peak support request times.
- Generate FAQs based on recent customer queries.
- Recommend training areas for support teams based on customer feedback.

12. Risk Management:

- Predict potential risks in our supply chain.
- Analyse factors influencing our business risks.
- Recommend strategies to mitigate specific risks.
- Evaluate the reliability of a new supplier or partner.
- Monitor online mentions for potential PR crises.

13. Ethics & Sustainability:

- Analyse the sustainability of our operations.
- Recommend steps to make our business eco-friendlier.
- Evaluate the ethical implications of a business decision.
- Monitor our carbon footprint over time.
- Suggest partnerships with eco-friendly brands or initiatives.

14. Remote Work & Collaboration:

- Recommend tools for efficient remote work.
- Analyse the productivity of remote vs. in-office teams.
- Suggest virtual team-building activities.
- Predict the need for remote infrastructure upgrades.
- Generate guidelines for effective virtual meetings.

15. Training & Development:

- Recommend online courses for specific skills.
- Generate a training schedule for a new hire.
- Evaluate the effectiveness of a training program.

- Suggest topics for the next team workshop.
- Predict future skill requirements in our industry.

16. Knowledge Management:

- Organise company documents for easy retrieval.
- Recommend tools for effective knowledge sharing.
- Analyse the usage and effectiveness of our internal knowledge base.
- Suggest ways to improve internal communication.
- Generate summaries of lengthy company reports.

17. Legal & Compliance:

- Monitor regulations that might impact our business.
- Recommend compliance measures for a new product.
- Evaluate the legal implications of a business contract.
- Generate a checklist for international business expansion.
- Monitor industry news for legal updates relevant to us.

18. Event Planning & Management:

- Recommend venues for our next corporate event.
- Predict the turnout for an event based on current RSVPs.
- Generate an event schedule.
- Recommend vendors or partners for an event.
- Evaluate feedback from an event.

19. Research & Development:

- Analyse trends in our industry.
- Recommend areas of research for product improvement.
- Evaluate the viability of a prototype.
- Predict the market response to a product modification.
- Generate hypotheses for a market research survey.

20. Communication & PR:

- Monitor online mentions of our brand.
- Recommend strategies to improve brand image.
- Evaluate the effectiveness of a PR campaign.
- Generate responses to common media queries.
- Analyse the sentiment of news articles mentioning our brand.

Top Tip - Remember, while these AI prompts are tailored to fit generic business needs, real effectiveness comes from customising prompts based on specific industry nuances and your unique organisational objectives. Use industry terminology to research for better results.

Test and adapt applicable 'prompts' to suit your business – By: type, industry sector, competitors, consumers, or queries.

Chapter 2: Crafting and Customising AI Prompts for Optimal Results

In the preceding chapter, we provided a robust list of AI prompts curated to address the various needs of businesses across diverse domains. While these generic prompts serve as a sturdy foundation, understanding the art of crafting and customising them ensures that businesses can tap into the AI's full potential.

In 2023, crafting AI prompts for business use, should focus on specificity and context-awareness to optimise decision-making and operational efficiency, while also incorporating ethical considerations to ensure responsible AI usage.

1. The Power of Specificity:

The first rule in effective AI prompt crafting is specificity. The more precise your instruction, the closer the AI's output will align with your desired outcome.

Example: Instead of asking, "Analyse market trends," you could specify, "Analyse market trends for electric cars in the European region from January to June 2023." as an example.

2. Context Matters:

Embedding the context within a prompt aids AI in understanding the broader picture, ensuring the response is relevant to the situation at hand.

Example: "Recommend marketing strategies" could be better framed as, "Recommend marketing strategies for our new vegan skincare range targeting millennials."

3. Limitations and Parameters:

By setting clear boundaries or guidelines, you can ensure the AI's output is manageable and directly usable.

Example: Instead of asking for "Content ideas for our blog," specify "Provide 5 content ideas for our tech blog focusing on emerging AI technologies." Be very specific with your use of prompts.

4. Iterative Questioning:

AI models can provide deeper insights when engaged in iterative querying, which involves breaking down a broad question into a sequence of narrower ones. It can use your data to analysis information regarding your business.

Example: Instead of "How can we improve customer satisfaction?", start with "What are the top 3 complaints from customers?", followed by "What solutions can address these complaints?"

5. Playing with Open-ended vs. Closed-ended Prompts:

The nature of your question can determine the structure of the AI's response. Open-ended prompts encourage more exploratory and extensive answers, while closed-ended one's lead to concise and direct outputs.

Example: "How can we optimise our supply chain?" (Open-ended) **vs.** "Is our current supply route cost-effective?" (Closed-ended).

6. Seeking Diverse Perspectives:

One of the unique advantages of AI is its ability to approach a problem from various angles. By tweaking your prompt, you can gather multiple perspectives on a single issue.

Example: "List the advantages of implementing a remote work policy" can be complemented with "List the challenges of implementing a remote work policy." See what I mean!

7. Continuous Refinement:

The process of prompt crafting is dynamic. It's crucial to monitor the effectiveness of your prompts regularly, refining them based on results and changing business needs.

Example: If "Predict next month's sales" isn't yielding accurate results, refine it to "Predict next month's sales based on the last three months' data and upcoming marketing campaigns."

How to Integrate Business Data to an AI System for Analysis and Future Advice?

Providing business data to an AI system for analysis and future advice is a multi-step process. It involves careful preparation of the data, selecting the right AI tools or platforms, and ensuring the whole process is carried out securely and ethically.

Here's a general roadmap to consider, edit and follow:

1. **Data Collection and Preparation:**
     - **Data Aggregation: Accumulate all business data from various sources, such as CRMs, ERPs, databases, and spreadsheets.**

- ◦ **Data Cleaning:** Ensure data is free from errors, inconsistencies, and duplicates. Clean data is vital for accurate analysis.
- ◦ **Data Transformation:** Convert data into a format suitable for AI processing. This could involve normalization, encoding categorical variables, or structuring data into tables.

2. **Security and Compliance:**
   - ◦ **Backup:** Before providing data to an AI system, always keep backups.
   - ◦ **Data Masking and Anonymisation:** Remove or alter personal or sensitive information to ensure data privacy. This is particularly vital if the AI processing happens on a cloud platform or an external system.
   - ◦ **Data Encryption:** Always encrypt data, both in transit (when sending to an AI system) and at rest (when stored).

3. **Choice of AI System:** (Professional Consultancy advice is recommended)
   - ◦ **Custom Solutions:** Develop in-house AI models tailored to specific business needs, using frameworks like TensorFlow or PyTorch.
   - ◦ **Pre-built Platforms:** Use platforms like IBM Watson, Google Cloud AI, or Azure Machine Learning, which offer pre-

trained models and tools for business analytics.

- Hybrid Approaches: Sometimes, a combination of custom and pre-built solutions may work best for your business.

4. Integration:
    - APIs: Most AI platforms provide APIs to feed data into their systems and fetch results.
    - Direct Database Integration: Some advanced platforms allow for direct database connections for real-time analysis.

5. Analysis and Training:
    - Supervised Learning: If you have labelled data (i.e., data with known outcomes), you can use it to train an AI model.
    - Unsupervised Learning: For data without labels, clustering or association algorithms might be applied to uncover hidden patterns.
    - Feedback Loop: As AI provides insights or advice, human experts should review the recommendations. This feedback can be used to refine and train the AI system for further analysis.

6. Interpreting Results:
    - Visualisation Tools: Tools like Tableau, PowerBI, or even libraries like Matplotlib

in Python can be used to visualise the AI's findings.

- Collaboration with Data Scientists: Ensure your team includes individuals skilled in AI and data interpretation to understand and leverage the AI's insights.

7. Regular Updates and Maintenance:
   - Update the Data: Regularly feed new business data into the AI system to keep the insights current and relevant. Train office staff to use AI system and inputs.
   - Model Re-training: As business evolves, the model might need re-training or fine-tuning to adapt to new data patterns.

1. Ethical Considerations:
   - Transparency: Ensure stakeholders know how the AI system makes decisions, especially if these decisions have significant business consequences.
   - Bias Check: Continuously monitor and correct for any biases in AI-generated insights or advice.

Lastly, while AI can provide valuable insights and predictions, it's crucial for business leaders to combine these findings with human expertise, intuition, and understanding of the broader business context, customer relationships and market sectors.

Conclusion:

Crafting effective AI prompts is as much an art as it is a science. With the right balance of specificity, context, and adaptability, businesses can optimise their interactions with AI, ensuring they glean the most value from this transformative technology.

As the realms of AI and business continue to intertwine, mastering this subtle art of communication will undoubtedly emerge as a crucial competency for business leaders of the future. The data that you use with any AI system must be clean and correct to ensure the best results.

Chapter 3: Integrating AI-Powered Insights into Business Strategy: A Roadmap for 2023/2024.

In previous chapters, we delved into the intricate art of crafting effective AI prompts and their pivotal role in harnessing the potential of AI for business.

However, generating valuable insights from AI is only half the battle. The real differentiator for businesses in 2023/2024 will be how they integrate these insights into actionable strategies.

This chapter will serve as a comprehensive roadmap for businesses to seamlessly weave AI-powered insights into a company's strategic fabric.

1. The Transition from Insight to Action:

Understanding the distinction between raw data, insights, and actionable steps is crucial. Here, we'll explore how to effectively transition from AI-generated insights to implementable actions.

2. Alignment with Business Goals:

No matter how revolutionary an insight might seem, it's redundant if it doesn't align with your business objectives. This section discusses methodologies to ensure that AI outputs are consistently in harmony with overarching business goals.

3. Stakeholder Engagement:

For AI-driven strategies to be successful, it's essential to have buy-in from all relevant stakeholders. We'll delve into communication strategies that highlight the value proposition of AI insights to different teams and decision-makers.

4. Piloting and Prototyping:

Before a full-fledged rollout of an AI-inspired strategy, piloting is essential. This segment will guide businesses on how to prototype and test strategies on a smaller scale, allowing for refinements based on real-world feedback.

5. Continuous Feedback Loops:

The dynamic nature of business requires a system where AI-generated strategies are constantly refined based on feedback. Here, we'll discuss setting up systems for continuous learning and adaptation.

6. Ethical Considerations:

Incorporating AI insights into business decisions brings along a host of ethical considerations. This section is dedicated to ensuring businesses make informed, ethical, and socially responsible decisions based on AI outputs.

7. Preparing for the Future:

With the pace of technological evolution, what's groundbreaking today might become obsolete tomorrow. This closing segment will focus on how businesses can stay agile, ensuring their AI-driven strategies evolve with changing times and technologies.

Conclusion:

As AI continues its upward trajectory in influencing business decisions, its integration into core business strategies becomes non-negotiable. This chapter provides a holistic guide for businesses to ensure that the transition from AI-generated insights to actionable business strategies is seamless, effective, and future ready.

Chapter 4: Measuring the ROI of AI-Driven Business Strategies:

A Data-Driven Approach for 2023/2024

While integrating AI-powered insights into your business strategy is crucial for staying competitive, quantifying the impact of these initiatives becomes equally vital.

This chapter takes you through the methods and metrics for effectively measuring the Return on Investment (ROI) of your AI-driven strategies.

With a data-driven lens, let's establish how you can attribute success to your AI endeavours and make informed decisions for the future.

1. The Importance of ROI Metrics:

Understanding the monetary impact of AI implementations is crucial for justifying the investment and planning future initiatives.

- **Clear Baselines:** Establish the performance metrics before AI implementation to have a clear comparison point.
- **Benchmarking:** Compare the outcomes with industry standards to evaluate the competitive edge your AI initiatives offer.

2. Types of ROI Metrics:

There are numerous ways to measure **ROI** depending on the area of application.

- **Cost Savings:** Reduction in operational costs due to automation.
- **Revenue Growth:** Increases in sales attributed to AI-driven marketing strategies.
- **Customer Satisfaction:** Measured through Net Promoter Scores (NPS) or Customer Satisfaction Scores (CSAT).

3. Time Horizon for ROI:

AI initiatives may have short-term or long-term impacts.

- **Immediate ROI:** Realised through automation and process efficiencies.
- **Long-term ROI:** Could be from brand-building or

customer retention strategies.

4. Qualitative Assessments:

Not all impacts are easily quantifiable.

- **Employee Satisfaction:** Reduced workload and streamlined processes often lead to happier employees.
- **Brand Perception:** Improved customer service can elevate the brand, though this is harder to measure numerically.

5. Periodic Review and Audits:

To accurately gauge ROI, periodic evaluations are essential.

- **Quarterly Reviews:** A shorter time frame for strategies that are expected to yield immediate results.
- **Annual Audits:** For long-term strategies like brand building or R&D innovations.

6. Challenges in Measuring ROI:

The multifaceted impact of AI can make ROI calculation complex.

- **Attribution:** Parsing out the specific influence of AI in multifactor successes.
- **Data Integrity:** Ensuring that the data used for ROI

calculations is accurate and up to date.

7. Future-Proofing ROI Measurement:

As AI evolves, so should your methods for measuring its impact.

- **Adaptive Metrics**: Be prepared to revise your KPIs as AI technologies advance.
- **Sustainability:** Consider the long-term sustainability of your AI initiatives as a component of ROI.

Implementing artificial intelligence (AI) can provide a company with a range of Return on Investment (ROI) benefits.

Listing of Potential ROI a Company Could Achieve:

Increased Efficiency: Automating routine tasks can lead to significant time savings, reducing the need for manual input and allowing employees to focus on more strategic tasks.

Cost Savings: Automating tasks can reduce labour costs. Moreover, AI can help in reducing operational costs by optimising processes.

Enhanced Decision Making: AI-driven analytics can help businesses make more informed decisions, leading to better outcomes and reduced risks.

Increased Sales: AI-driven recommendation systems, personalised marketing campaigns, and sales predictions can boost sales figures.

Improved Customer Experience: Chatbots, personalised content, and faster response times can enhance the customer journey, leading to increased customer loyalty and higher retention rates.

New Revenue Streams: AI can enable new products, services, or business models. For instance, an e-commerce business might develop a personalised shopping assistant feature by using AI.

Reduced Errors: AI can analyse vast amounts of data with high precision, leading to reduced human errors in processes like data entry or analysis.

Enhanced Productivity: AI tools can help employees work more productively by providing insights, automating repetitive tasks, or aiding in complex problem-solving.

Predictive Maintenance: For businesses with machinery or infrastructure, AI can predict when equipment is likely to fail, leading to reduced downtime and maintenance costs.

Risk Management: AI can assist in fraud detection, credit scoring, and assessing other potential risks, helping businesses minimise potential financial losses.

Supply Chain and Inventory Management: AI can forecast demand, optimise inventory levels, and streamline logistics, reducing holding costs and improving service levels.

Personalisation at Scale: AI can tailor product offerings, content, and marketing strategies to individual user preferences on a massive scale.

Better R&D: AI can accelerate research & development processes, leading to faster innovation and reduced time-to-market for new products or services.

Enhanced Talent Management: AI-driven HR tools can better match job candidates to roles, predict which employees might leave the company, or personalise training programs.

Optimised Marketing: AI can enhance marketing strategies by segmenting audiences more effectively, optimising online ad bids, predicting the success of campaigns, and personalising content and email marketing for better engagement.

Competitive Advantage: Early adoption and effective implementation of AI can provide an edge over other competitors.

Scalability: Once AI models are trained, they can often handle vast amounts of data or tasks without linear increases in costs, allowing businesses to scale operations efficiently.

Sustainability: AI can optimise energy use in operations, predict renewable energy supply, and improve resource allocation, supporting a company's sustainability goals.

It's essential to note that the actual ROI achieved from implementing AI will vary based on the industry, the specific application, the quality of the AI solution, and the company's ability to integrate and leverage the technology effectively.

Conclusion:

Measuring the ROI of AI-driven business strategies is a nuanced, ongoing process that requires both quantitative and qualitative evaluations.

With the right framework, businesses can assess the success of their AI initiatives in the context of both immediate and long-term objectives.

As we tread deeper into 2023/2024, this data-driven understanding will prove invaluable for steering strategic directions, securing stakeholder buy-in, investments and achieving sustainable growth.

Chapter 5: Future-Ready Framework: Sustaining AI-Driven Business Innovations Beyond 2023/ 2024.

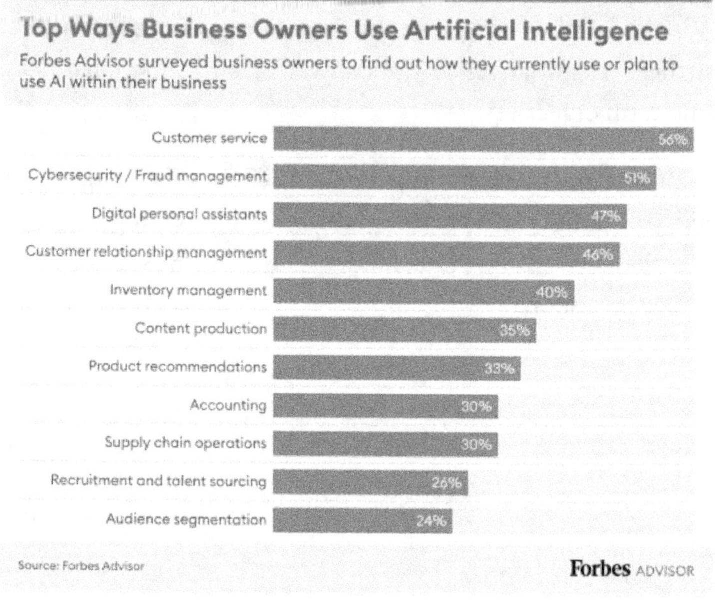

As businesses fine-tune their strategies to leverage AI effectively and gauge ROI, the next critical question becomes sustainability.

How do you ensure that the AI-driven strategies you've implemented today will continue to provide value in the future?

This chapter delves into creating a framework that is adaptable, scalable, and ready to meet the business challenges beyond 2023/2024.

1. The Dynamics of Technological Evolution:

Recognising the pace at which AI and related technologies are advancing is the first step in future-proofing your strategies.

- **Continuous Learning:** Commit to keeping abreast of technological advancements in the AI field.
- **Partnerships:** Forge alliances with tech companies and thought leaders to stay ahead.

2. Adaptable Business Models:

To remain sustainable, your business model needs to accommodate the fast-changing landscape of AI software and tech.

- **Modular Design:** Implement a business model that can easily incorporate new technologies or methodologies. Use software platforms that can integrate with business models.
- **Diversification:** Diversify your AI applications across different areas of your business to minimise risk.

3. Scalability:

Your AI applications should be designed to grow with your business.

- **Infrastructure:** Invest in a cloud infrastructure that can handle increasing data and computational needs.
- **Human Capital:** Employ or train staff who can manage and optimise AI systems at scale.

4. Data Governance and Ethics:

As your AI initiatives grow, ethical considerations and data governance become increasingly complex yet important.

- **Ethics Committee:** Form a team focused on assessing the ethical implications of your AI strategies.
- **Transparency:** Maintain transparent practices, especially in data collection and processing.

5. Resilience and Contingency Planning:

AI applications are not foolproof and require backup plans.

- **Redundancies:** Build failsafe's into your AI systems to handle disruptions.
- **Disaster Recovery:** Develop a robust plan for data recovery and system reactivation.

6. Long-Term Financial Planning:

Sustainability also hinges on long-term financial feasibility.

- **Budgeting:** Factor in not just initial implementation costs, but also long-term maintenance and upgrading.
- **Revenue Streams:** Look for ways to monetize your AI capabilities, perhaps by offering them as services to other businesses.

7. Monitoring and Updating:

The sustainability of any system relies on continual monitoring and timely updates.

- **Performance Metrics:** Regularly assess key performance indicators to measure the sustainability of your AI initiatives.
- **Updates:** Systematic updates are crucial to maintaining the efficacy and security of your AI applications.

Compiled and published in 2023, website **FinanceOnline.com** produced important and informative statistics regarding AI advancements in the Business sectors. I would recommend you take a read of -

Worth a Read - *70 Vital Artificial Intelligence Statistics: 2023 Data Analysis & Market Share* ... Published by Finance Online – link below:

Website - https://financesonline.com/artificial-intelligence-statistics/

Conclusion:

As the business landscape continues to evolve, long-term sustainability becomes the cornerstone of success.

By focusing on adaptability, ethics, scalability, and resilience, businesses can ensure that their AI-driven strategies remain effective and impactful beyond 2023.

For the future, the sustainability of your businesses AI initiatives will be a dynamic endeavour, requiring ongoing attention and adjustment to navigate an ever-changing technological terrain successfully.

On a side note, I recently (Aug 23) published an eBook entitled, **Green Business - People - Planet - Profit - 2023/24:**[1]

A Comprehensive Guide to Building & Managing A Sustainable Business which explores and documents in detail the principles, strategies, and practices that embody running a sustainable business.

Aiming to equip businesspeople with the knowledge and tools necessary to embark on this essential greener business path.

---

1. https://shorturl.at/koSW2

Available on Amazon and other online book retailers.

Chapter 6: Talent Management in the AI Era: Navigating the Intersection of Human and Machine Intelligence ...

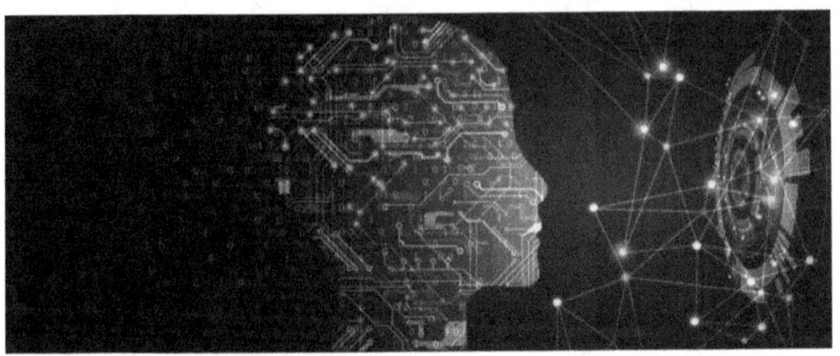

Hi vs Ai ...

In an age where Artificial Intelligence (AI) is revolutionising industries, it's easy to overlook one of the most impacted realms: human resources (HI) and talent management.

The AI era presents an intriguing dichotomy; while it automates several tasks, it also necessitates a workforce that's skilled in harnessing this automation.

This chapter delves into how businesses can navigate the complexities of talent management in this AI-driven landscape.

1. Talent Acquisition:

Recruiting in the AI era is no longer just about skills; it's also about adaptability and familiarity with technology.

AI-Screening Tools: Using AI to parse through resumes, match skills, and even conduct initial interviews.

Skills Assessment: Identifying the 'AI readiness' of candidates through specialised tests and interviews.

2. Using AI for Onboarding and Training:

New Hires: Integrating new hires into an AI-imbued environment requires a distinct approach.

AI-Led Onboarding: Utilising AI tools to make the onboarding process smooth and informative.

Training Modules: Implement AI in training programs to provide real-time feedback and adapt to individual learning styles.

3. Performance Monitoring:

AI can provide insightful metrics, but the human touch remains essential.

Data-Driven Reviews: Utilising AI-generated analytics for more objective performance evaluations.

Human Element: Ensuring that AI-generated metrics are supplemented with qualitative assessments from supervisors.

4. Employee Engagement and Satisfaction:

Harness AI to improve the overall employee experience.

Sentiment Analysis: Use AI algorithms to gauge the mood and engagement level of employees through regular surveys.

Work-Life Balance: AI can automate repetitive tasks, freeing employees to focus on more rewarding aspects of their jobs.

5. Upskilling and Reskilling:

In a fast-evolving landscape, continuous learning is a must.

AI-Based Learning Platforms: Implement platforms that offer tailored learning paths for employees.

Certification Programs: Offer AI-related certification programs to keep the workforce updated.

6. AI Ethics and Fairness:

Incorporating AI into HR processes raises ethical questions that need addressing.

Bias in AI: Be cautious of algorithmic biases in recruitment and evaluation processes.

Transparency: Keep employees informed about the extent and objectives of AI usage in HR.

7. Talent Retention:

The AI era changes not just how you attract talent, but also how you retain it.

Predictive Analytics: Use AI to predict which employees are most likely to leave and take pre-emptive actions.

Tailored Benefits: Use AI to tailor benefits packages based on employee needs and preferences.

Conclusion:

Navigating talent management in the AI era is a complex but rewarding endeavour. By integrating AI judiciously into various aspects of human resources—from recruitment to retention—***businesses can optimise their most critical asset - their people.***

As we venture further into 2023 and 2024, it becomes increasingly clear that the fusion of human intelligence with artificial intelligence holds the key to an organisation's long-term success.

Chapter 7: AI in Customer Experience: Elevating Engagement and Loyalty Through Intelligent Interactions

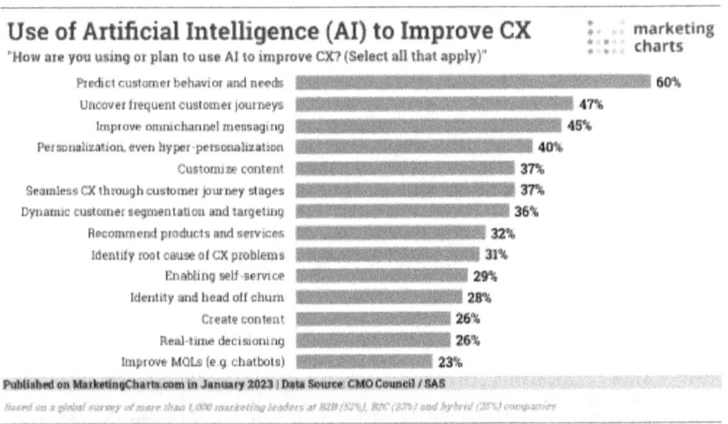

In the age of digital transformation, the customer experience (CX) stands at the forefront of business success.

AI technologies offer unprecedented ways to not only understand customer behaviours and preferences but also to automate and enhance interactions.

This chapter explores how businesses can leverage AI to improve CX, deepening customer relationships and driving brand loyalty.

1. Customer Service Automation:

AI-powered chatbots and virtual assistants are redefining customer service.

- **Chatbots:** Use chatbots for initial interactions, frequently asked questions, and real-time assistance.
- **Virtual Assistants:** Deploy more advanced AI systems for personalised recommendations and in-depth support. Handle customer queries 24/7, offer instant support, and direct complex issues to human agents.

2. Personalisation at Scale:

AI enables hyper-personalisation, which is crucial for customer engagement.

- **Dynamic Content:** Utilise AI to serve personalised content based on user behaviours, preferences, and past interactions.
- **Product Recommendations:** Implement AI algorithms to recommend products or services tailored to individual customers.

3. Data-Driven Insights:

Harness the power of AI analytics to understand customer behaviours.

- **Collect Data:** Begin by collecting relevant data from your customer interactions – chat logs, purchase history, feedback, etc. Ensure that the data collected is accurate, of high quality, and respects privacy.

- **Customer Segmentation:** Use AI to categorise customers based on buying behaviour, preferences, and other commercial factors.
- **Predictive Analytics:** Utilise AI to forecast customer needs and future behaviours.

4. Voice Search and Voice Assistants:

Voice technology offers a more natural, convenient way for customers to interact with your business.

- **Voice Search Optimization:** Prepare your digital platforms for voice search by utilizing AI-powered tools.
- **Voice-Activated Customer Service:** Integrate voice assistants to help customers navigate your services.

5. Augmented Reality (AR) Experiences:

Enhance in-store and online experiences through AR powered by AI.

- **Virtual Try-On:** Use AR for virtual fitting rooms or product trials.
- **In-Store Navigation:** Deploy AR for intelligent in-store guidance and information.

6. Real-Time Customer Feedback:

AI can help collect and analyse customer feedback instantly.

- **Sentiment Analysis:** Deploy AI algorithms to assess customer reviews and social media interactions.
- **Automated Surveys:** Use AI to administer post-interaction surveys for immediate feedback.

7. AI Ethics and Transparency:

Transparency is key when AI is used in customer-facing applications.

- **Data Privacy:** Clearly inform customers how their data will be used and stored.
- **Algorithmic Fairness:** Ensure your AI algorithms are unbiased and provide equal service to all customers. Implement robust data protection and cybersecurity measures.

Conclusion:

Incorporating AI into the customer experience journey allows for a more personalised, efficient, and engaging interaction that can lead to increased customer satisfaction and loyalty.

However, it's crucial that businesses also maintain ethical standards, especially in terms of data privacy, all legal regulations and algorithmic fairness.

As we continue through 2023/2024, the fusion of AI technologies and customer experience is set to redefine the landscape of customer engagement and loyalty, offering vast opportunities for businesses willing to adapt and innovate using AI powered software tools.

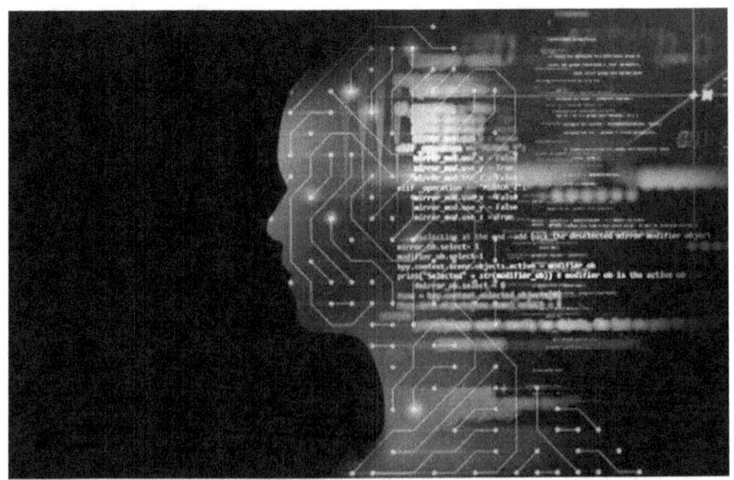

Chapter 8: AI and Competitive Advantage: Outsmarting the Market through Intelligent Strategies

In today's business environment, having a competitive edge is more crucial than ever. But how do you maintain this edge in a world increasingly influenced by Artificial Intelligence?

As AI permeates various sectors, its potential to create a competitive advantage is becoming increasingly evident. This chapter examines ways in which AI can strategically position businesses ahead of their competition.

A **2023 survey** of senior company leadership teams by **Investopedia**, stated that –

"Many chief executives think artificial intelligence (AI) will give them the upper hand in the future, though they are split on whether it will increase or decrease their human workforces."

KEY TAKEAWAYS

- Half of CEOs are starting to use AI in their operations, but fewer than a third have considered the impact that AI could have on their workforce.
- Generative AI will create workforce reductions or redeployment, said 43% of CEOs, while another 46% said AI would prompt them to hire additional workers.
- AI will help 43% of organisations make strategic decisions and another 36% will use the technology

for operational decisions.

- Investopedia issue regular business reports including on AI for Business, which you can read for free at their website - https://www.investopedia.com

1. Strategic Decision Making:

AI's analytical prowess is reshaping how companies make informed decisions.

- **Predictive Analysis:** Utilise AI to forecast market trends and customer behaviours to make informed decisions.
- **Real-Time Monitoring:** Leverage AI to keep track of competitors' activities and adjust your strategy accordingly.

2. Process Automation:

Automating mundane tasks is just the tip of the iceberg; AI's true potential lies in optimizing complex processes.

- **Workflow Automation:** Employ AI to enhance internal workflows, from procurement to product delivery.
- **Quality Control:** Use AI-based algorithms to ensure high-quality products, reducing errors and recalls.

3. Supply Chain Optimisation:

AI's impact on the supply chain is a game-changer for competitiveness.

- **Demand Forecasting:** Implement AI algorithms to anticipate product demand and manage inventory.
- **Logistics:** Utilise AI to optimise shipping routes, reducing costs and environmental impact.

4. Customer Relationship Management (CRM):

CRM systems powered by AI provide unprecedented levels of personalisation and customer engagement.

- **Automated Interactions:** Deploy AI to manage customer emails, online chat, and even phone calls.
- **Behavioural Tracking:** Use AI to map out customer journeys, identifying opportunities for up-selling and cross-selling opportunities.

5. Marketing and Advertising:

AI enables marketing strategies that are both efficient and personalised.

- **Ad Optimisation:** Employ AI algorithms to optimise online ad placements and bidding in real-time using Google Ads, Facebook/Instagram Ads, Twitter Ads, LinkedIn Ads, Bing Ads, and others.
- **Content Generation:** Use AI tools for generating advertising copy, social media posts, or even video content. Generate ideas for the sales and marketing teams to brainstorm.

6. Talent and Human Capital:

Your people are a significant source of competitive advantage; AI can help you manage them more effectively.

- **Talent Scouting:** Use AI to sift through candidate's CV's, identifying those who fit your company's needs and culture.
- **Employee Retention:** Leverage AI to predict employee turnover and identify ways to improve job satisfaction.
- **Measure & Celebrate Success:** Monitor key performance indicators (KPIs) that align with your objectives. Celebrate and share success stories to build internal support for further AI investments.

7. Ethical Considerations:

Gaining a competitive advantage through AI should not compromise ethical standards.

- **Data Security:** Ensure robust security measures to protect sensitive data.
- **Fair Competition:** Utilise AI in a way that promotes fair competition and adheres to antitrust and all business laws.

Conclusion:

Artificial Intelligence offers a myriad of ways to gain and sustain a competitive advantage.

From enhancing decision-making to optimising supply chains and personalising customer interactions, AI has the potential to significantly outpace traditional business strategies.

However, this advantage is not without its ethical and legal considerations, which businesses must diligently consider and address.

As we navigate through 2023/2024 and beyond, companies that successfully integrate AI into their competitive strategy, are likely to emerge as leaders in their respective markets or at least have an improved success strategy and plan.

Chapter 9: Global Considerations for AI in Business:

Navigating Cultural, Regulatory, and Economic Landscapes

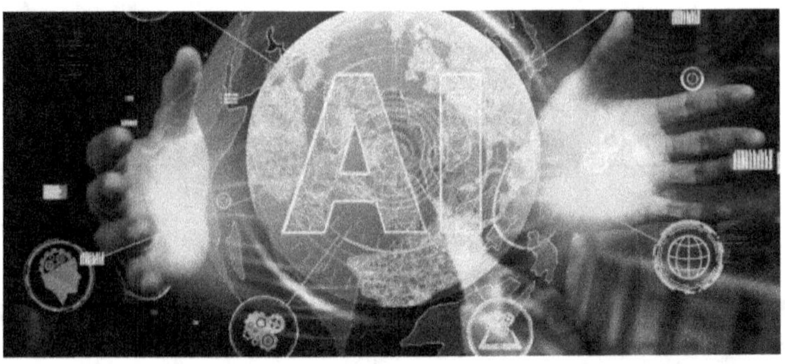

As AI technologies continue to evolve and proliferate, their applications are increasingly being adopted across international markets.

However, going global with AI is not just a matter of scaling; it involves a complex interplay of cultural, regulatory, and economic considerations. This chapter aims to guide businesses on how to navigate these complexities when deploying AI strategies on a global scale.

1. Cultural Sensitivity and Localisation:

Understanding cultural nuances is critical when implementing AI in different countries.

Language and Communication: Use AI-powered translation and localisation services to adapt your business offerings.

Consumer Behaviour: Leverage AI to analyse and adapt to local buying habits and preferences.

2. Regulatory Compliance:

Different nations have distinct regulations concerning data privacy, cybersecurity, and AI ethics.

Data Privacy Laws: Familiarise yourself with GDPR in Europe, CCPA in California, and other regional data protection regulations.

Ethical Guidelines: Adhere to local and international ethical standards for AI, such as avoiding bias in algorithms.

3. Economic Considerations:

Currency fluctuations, tax laws, and trade tariffs can impact your AI implementation.

Cost Optimisation: Use AI to forecast economic trends and adjust your pricing and spending strategies accordingly.

Supply Chain Management: Consider economic factors like tariffs and taxes when optimising your AI-driven supply chain on a global scale.

4. Talent Management:

Skilled personnel in AI are essential; however, talent pools vary from region to region. Consider upskilling key people within the business in AI technology.

Remote Teams: Leverage AI tools to manage and coordinate remote teams spread across different time zones, if applicable.

Local Expertise: Use AI algorithms to identify skill gaps in local markets and tailor your recruitment strategies to attract key talent.

5. Partnering and Collaboration:

Strategic partnerships can help businesses adapt their AI technologies to regional or local needs.

Joint Ventures: Use AI to identify potential business partners who can help adapt your technology to meet local requirements and/or increase business opportunities and revenues.

Cross-Border Innovation: Leverage AI to collaborate on research and development projects that have global applications.

6. Market-Specific AI Solutions:

Not all AI applications will be universally successful; customisation is key.

Product Adaptation: Use AI algorithms to modify your product features according to the preferences of different regional markets.

Service Localisation: Utilise AI to tailor your customer service and support to local languages and even country specific customs.

7. Ethical and Social Implications:

The social fabric of each market will react differently to the use of AI technologies.

AI and Employment: Be conscious of how AI adoption may affect employment rates in different regions.

Cultural Attitudes: Use AI to study cultural sentiments towards technology and innovation, adapting your strategies accordingly.

Conclusion:

Expanding AI strategies to a global, national, or even at local level business markets, is a multifaceted challenge that requires careful consideration of cultural, regulatory, and economic factors.

It's crucial to adapt and localise AI applications to meet the needs and restrictions of different world markets.

As we progress through 2023/2024, companies that successfully implement a globally, nationally, or locally sensitive AI strategy, will not only benefit from new market opportunities, but also contribute positively to different communities worldwide.

Chapter 10: Security Concerns & Mitigations in AI: Safeguarding Business in the Intelligent Era.

I think we can all agreed that the increasing adoption of Artificial Intelligence in business activities brings about new opportunities for innovation and efficiencies.

However, like any new wide-spread innovation, it also introduces a host of security concerns that could potentially jeopardise the very advantages AI offers.

This chapter aims to shed light on these concerns and offer mitigation strategies to ensure that your AI-driven business remains secure and trustworthy.

1. Data Privacy:

Handling and storing vast amounts of data, come with significant privacy and security risks.

- **Encryption:** Utilise strong encryption algorithms to protect data at rest, in transit, and during processing. Research professional software applications to protect business data.
- **Access Control:** Use AI to monitor and manage who has access to sensitive data.
- **Concern:** AI systems require large amounts of data, some of which could be sensitive. Unauthorised access can lead to data breaches or leaks.

Advice:

- Implement robust encryption techniques for data at rest, in transit, and during processing.
- Regularly update security protocols and ensure compliance with regulations like GDPR, HIPAA or similar.
- Provide adequate training for management and staff to ensure every aspect of the business is protected and operates within all legal and ethical frameworks.
- Decide who within the organisation has access to business systems.

2. Adversarial Attacks:

AI systems can be vulnerable to sophisticated attacks that exploit their learning algorithms and data.

- **Data Poisoning:** Be vigilant about the data used to train your AI models, ensuring it is clean and trustworthy.

- **Robust Modelling:** Implement AI models that are resistant to adversarial inputs.

Concern: Attackers can feed malicious data into AI models to skew results or make them behave unpredictably.

Advice: Implement robustness checks to identify and filter out adversarial inputs. Continuously update the model to adapt to new kinds of security attacks.

3. Identity and Authentication:

AI can both aid and hinder identity verification processes.

- **Biometric Authentication:** Use AI-driven biometric systems for secure authentication.
- **Multi-Factor Authentication (MFA):** Implement AI-enhanced MFA to add layers of security.

Concern: Employees with access to AI models and data, can misuse them.

Advice: Limit access to AI systems to those who genuinely need it and monitor for unauthorised or suspicious activities.

- **Educate employees** about the importance of AI security and legal rules and procedures. Prepare a company – Standard

Operation Procedures (SOP) to detail and inform all staff of all rules regarding AI usage and company data.

4. Phishing and Social Engineering:

AI can mimic human behaviours, making 'phishing attacks' more convincing.

- **Behavioural Analysis:** Use AI to detect unusual patterns in user or customer behaviours or online correspondence that may indicate a phishing attempt.
- **Employee Training:** Employ AI-driven training modules to educate staff on the risks of social engineering and security challenges in the age of AI.

Concern: AI models can inadvertently introduce or perpetuate bias, leading to possible unfair or discriminatory decisions.

Advice: Audit all AI models for bias and fairness regularly. Use diverse training data and explicitly train models to be unbiased where possible. Professional consultants maybe required to assist and advise with this.

5. Surveillance and Monitoring:

AI-driven surveillance systems can be both a boon and a bane for any business.

- **Activity Monitoring:** Utilise AI algorithms to detect

unusual activity or vulnerabilities in your network and finance departments. AI systems could also be used for types of employee monitoring and productivity.

- **Ethical Guidelines:** Ensure your monitoring adheres to all privacy, business laws and ethical considerations to all employees.

Concern: Use of AI surveillance for employee monitoring, can raise ethical concerns about autonomy, privacy, HR, and ongoing legal concerns and trust from employees.

Advice: Be transparent with employees about the extent and purpose of any AI monitoring.

Develop a clear HR policy that is communicated to all stakeholders and make sure to obtain informed consent if necessary. All businesses must abide by all country specific employment, data and privacy laws and any other business regulations.

The business may require professional legal and HR advice and/or revised staff policies and documentation, if implementing any AI lead employee surveillance.

By addressing these concerns proactively, businesses can more effectively and ethically utilise AI in surveillance and monitoring, reducing risks, financial or other losses and improving productivity, health & safety, and security for the overall business, including its employees, suppliers, and customers.

6. Regulatory Compliance:

Keeping up with the evolving landscape of cybersecurity regulations is critical.

- **Compliance Checkers:** Use AI to automate the tracking of regulatory changes and ensure full compliance.
- **Audit Trails:** Implement AI systems that can produce robust logs for auditing purposes.

7. Disaster Recovery and Incident Response:

AI can expedite the recovery process following a security incident.

- **Incident Prediction:** Use AI to predict possible points of failure or attack, enabling proactive defences.
- **Automated Response:** Employ AI algorithms to automate responses to certain types of security incidents, minimising damage, and alerting management.

Conclusion:

Security and privacy are a paramount concern in the age of AI, requiring a nuanced and multi-layered approach to safeguard data, customer and employee identities, and business systems.

While AI itself poses new types of security risks, it can also be part of the solution when used intelligently.

As we advance through 2023/2024, businesses that prioritise security in their AI strategies will be better positioned to protect their assets and maintain the trust of their staff, clients, and partners.

Chapter 11: The Future of AI in Business: Trends, Opportunities, and Challenges Beyond 2023/2024

Artificial Intelligence is a dynamic field, continually evolving and adapting. While it is crucial to understand the current applications and implications of AI in business, as outlined in previous chapters, it is equally important to consider the future landscape.

This chapter aims to explore emerging trends, potential opportunities, and challenges that businesses should prepare for as we move beyond the immediate horizon of 2023/2024.

1. Trends in AI Technology:

Technological advancements are accelerating at an exponential rate.

- **Quantum Computing:** The development of quantum computers could revolutionise AI capabilities.
- **Decentralised AI:** Blockchain and other decentralised technologies may offer new approaches to data integrity and model training.

2. Emerging Business Models:

AI will enable new ways of conducting business that we can't yet fully envision yet.

- **AI as a Service (AIaaS):** Outsourcing AI functionalities could become a norm.
- **AI-First Businesses:** Future companies might be built entirely around AI technologies.

3. The Role of Human Expertise:

AI will augment, not replace, human intelligence.

- **Human-AI Collaboration:** Future workspaces will likely involve humans and AI systems working in tandem for better co-efficiency.
- **Upskilling:** Education and training will evolve to help human workers better collaborate with AI systems, to use for improving business operations.

4. The Ethics of AI:

Ethical considerations will only grow more complex as AI becomes more sophisticated.

- **Explainability and Transparency:** Businesses will need to find ways to make complex AI decisions understandable to consumers and regulators.
- **Bias and Fairness:** Ethical AI that is free from human biases will remain a high-priority concern.

5. Globalisation and Geopolitical Impact:

AI will play a significant role in global economics and politics.

- **Data Sovereignty:** The geopolitical implications of data ownership will be a crucial concern for international businesses.
- **Global Industry Standards:** The international governmental and business communities may establish common standards for AI development, usage, and ethics over time.

6. Environmental Sustainability:

AI could either be a saviour or a strain on environmental resources.

- **Optimised Resource Usage:** AI could help companies use resources more efficiently, reducing wastage.
- **Carbon Footprint:** The computational requirements of large AI models could contribute to environmental degradation.

7. Preparing for the Future:

All Businesses, large and small, must adapt to stay ahead in the rapidly evolving landscape.

- **Continuous Learning:** Adopt a culture of ongoing education and adaptability.
- **Strategic Partnerships:** Collaborate with academic institutions, think tanks, business groups and other businesses to stay at the forefront of AI innovation.
- **Regulation:** There is already many tech leaders

calling for specific regulations for AI systems. In May 23, Sam Altman, the CEO of OpenAI, the company behind ChatGPT, testified before a US Senate committee, describing the potential pitfalls of the new technology.

In April 23, Elon Musk told the BBC: "I think there should be a regulatory body established for overseeing AI to make sure that it does not present a danger to the public."

Conclusion:

While the full impact of AI's future developments remains unknown, proactive preparation and strategic thinking will be key to navigating the challenges and opportunities ahead.

As we move beyond 2023/2024, the companies that continue to innovate, adapt, and consider the broader implications of AI will be the ones that thrive in this exciting new era.

"Like any new technology advancement, fortunes will be gained and lost ..."

Chapter 12: A Comprehensive List of Powerful AI Prompts to Use for Business.

As the title of this publication suggests, to get the very best results and unique insights from any AI system, you must consider what 'Prompts' you use.

I have researched and test hundreds of different types of AI prompts, to help get you started and improve your own prompting skills.

Try them for yourself and tweak them to suit your requirements, business type or commercial sectors.

Happy Prompting - It's always informative and educational ...

Useful Sample AI Prompts for Business Use.

AI Prompts for Business Use – as of Sep 2023:

Example - Using Long-from Detailed Prompts for Blog Posts or Content Ideas.

"I'm looking for a [type of blog post] that will engage my [ideal customer persona] with a unique and compelling perspective on [subject] and persuade them to take [desired action] on my [website/product]."

"I am searching for a blog post that can connect with my ideal customer persona in a way that feels unique and compelling. I want to provide them with a new perspective on the subject matter that will be interesting and engaging enough to persuade them to act on my website or product.

"I need a [type of blog post] that will provide valuable and relevant information to my [ideal customer persona] and persuade them to take [desired action] on my [website/product]."

"I require a blog post that can offer valuable and relevant information to my ideal customer persona. I want to be able to persuade them to act on my website or product using the information provided.

"I'm looking for a [type of blog post] that will educate my [ideal customer persona] on a specific [topic] and persuade them to take [desired action] on my [website/product]."

"I am in search of a blog post that can educate my ideal customer persona on a specific topic. I want to be able to persuade them to act on my website or product through the knowledge and information provided.

"I need a [type of blog post] that will speak directly to the needs and pain points of my [ideal customer persona] and persuade them to take [desired action] with a sense of urgency and strong offer."

"I require a blog post that can address the specific needs and pain points of my ideal customer persona. I want to be able to persuade them to take action on my website or product through a sense of urgency and a strong offer.

"I'm looking for a [type of blog post] that will showcase the value and benefits of my [product/service] to [ideal customer persona] and convince them to take [desired action] with social proof and credibility-building elements."

"I am searching for a blog post that can showcase the value and benefits of my product or service to my ideal customer persona. I want to be able to persuade them to take action on my website or product using social proof and credibility-building elements.

AI prompts can be a powerful way to elicit information, automate tasks, and derive insights across various departments in a business setting.

Listed below are 50 professional shortform AI prompts to consider, tailored for main business departments.

As sampled in the previous longform prompts, test and amend each prompt to suit your unique business and industry, by adding extra information and requests within a prompt, will result in a better-informed AI response:

Some prompts will require specific business information to be inputted for analysis by an AI system to give in depth feedback.

Customer Service:

"Automate the sorting of customer service tickets by priority."

"Generate responses to frequently asked questions."

"Identify recurring issues in customer complaints."

"Recommend improvements for our customer service processes."

Finance:

"Audit expense claims for compliance with company policy."

"Automate expense tracking and categorisation."

"Calculate the ROI of our recent marketing campaigns."

"Predict cash flow for the next quarter."

Human Resources:

"Analyse employee satisfaction survey results."

"Automate the initial screening of job applicants."

"Identify the skills gap within our organisation."

"Recommend training programs for employee development."

IT:

"Automate the backup of critical business data."

"Generate a list of outdated software and recommend updates."

"Monitor system performance and suggest optimisations."

"Scan for security vulnerabilities in our software."

Legal:

"Analyse risks in our intellectual property portfolio."

"Automate the tracking of legal obligations and deadlines."

"Identify potential compliance issues in contractual agreements."

"Recommend updates to company policies based on new legislation."

Marketing:

"Analyse customer sentiment from the last quarter's social media mentions."

"Automate the categorisation of customer complaints and queries."

"Generate suggestions for improving email open rates."

"Identify emerging market trends based on consumer search behaviour."

Operations:

"Analyse supplier performance metrics."

"Generate a maintenance schedule for machinery."

"Optimise warehouse stock based on historical sales data."

"Suggest ways to reduce operational costs."

R&D:

"Analyse market demand for potential new products."

"Generate ideas for feature improvements."

"Identify technology trends that could impact our industry."

"Optimise testing procedures for new product development."

Sales:

"Analyse competitor pricing strategies."

"Generate a weekly sales forecast."

"Provide a list of high-value prospects based on historical data."

"Recommend cross-selling opportunities for current customers."

"Identify key decision-makers within target organizations based on social media activity."

"Analyse the success rate of different sales strategies used in the past year."

"Recommend the best time of day to reach out to prospects based on historical engagement data."

"Generate a list of customers at risk of churn and suggest retention strategies."

Chapter 13 - Preparing for an AI-Augmented Business Future

As we conclude this comprehensive exploration of Artificial Intelligence in the business landscape, it's clear that we stand at the cusp of a transformative era.

Whether it's in automating routine processes, optimising supply chains, augmenting human decision-making, or even revolutionising customer experiences, AI's possibilities are virtually endless and will only advance as time goes by.

However, the incorporation of AI into business practices is not without its pitfalls. Ethical considerations around data privacy, algorithmic bias, and job displacement are just a few of the challenges that we will continue to wrestle with in the years ahead.

Consultants such as **Deloitte** and others like **KPMG, McKinsey & Company, Accenture** have already published several interesting reports regarding AI and the future of business.

You can access this content by visiting their websites. Sample links below to review.

https://www2.deloitte.com/content/dam/Deloitte/us/Documents/process-and-operations/us-ai-institute-future-of-ai.pdf

https://www.mckinsey.com/capabilities/quantumblack/our-insights

https://www.accenture.com/ie-en/insights/artificial-intelligence-summary-index

Note: The author has no affiliation to any of the above companies or services or providers mentioned within this publication. Website links only provided for informational purposes only. It is up to each reader to make their own informed decisions in using any business services provider. Do your research.

Chapter 14 - Last Thoughts - Asking Chat GPT.... AI Vs Humans!

I decide to ask **Chat GPT** the following question regarding - **Humans Versus AI**, below is what ChatGPT replied (as of Sep 2023):

Q. What are the differences between using AI in business versus Humans?

Answer:

Using AI and humans in business settings each come with their distinct advantages and disadvantages.

Here's a comparative look at both:

Using AI in Business

Advantages:

Efficiency: AI algorithms can process large sets of data much faster than a human, automating various tasks and leading to greater efficiency.

Scalability: AI systems can easily scale to meet the demands of growing data or workload, something that's much harder and costlier with human labour.

Data Analysis: Advanced AI algorithms can analyse data patterns and make forecasts with high levels of accuracy, which is particularly useful for tasks like market analysis, customer segmentation, and predictive maintenance.

Availability: *AI systems can operate 24/7 without the need for breaks, holidays, or sleep, making them particularly useful for tasks that require constant vigilance.*

Consistency: *AI systems perform tasks the same way every time, ensuring a high level of quality and reliability in output, unlike humans who can be inconsistent due to various factors like mood, health, and fatigue.*

Disadvantages: (From Chat GPT)

Cost: *The initial setup and ongoing maintenance of AI systems can be expensive.*

Complexity: *Implementing AI solutions often requires specialized expertise, which might not be readily available.*

Ethical and Legal Concerns: *Issues surrounding data privacy, security, and bias can be complex to navigate.*

Limited Creativity: *AI lacks the creativity and intuition that humans bring to problem-solving and strategic thinking.*

Job Displacement: *Automation through AI could lead to job losses in certain sectors.*

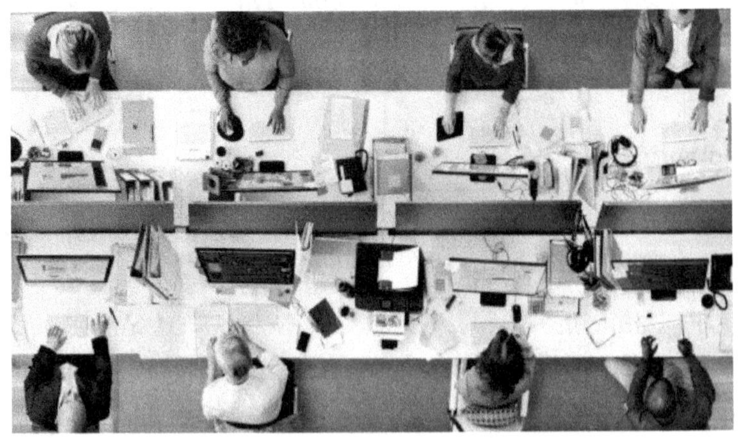

Using Humans in Business (From Chat GPT)

Advantages -

Creativity: *Humans excel at tasks that require creativity, innovative thinking, and adaptability.*

Emotional Intelligence: *Humans have the ability to understand and interpret social and emotional cues, which is vital for tasks like negotiation, customer service, and team collaboration.*

Ethical Judgement: *Humans have the ability to make value-based decisions, understanding the ethical and social implications of their actions.*

Contextual Understanding: *Unlike AI, humans can easily understand and interpret context, whether it's in conversation, problem-solving, or decision-making.*

Learning from Unstructured Data: *Humans are generally better at learning from unstructured data and experiences, without the need for large datasets.*

Disadvantages:

Cost: *Human labour is expensive. Salaries, benefits, and other employee-related costs can add up quickly.*

Errors and Inconsistency: *Humans are prone to mistakes and their performance can vary due to factors like fatigue, stress, and illness.*

Limited Data Processing: *Humans can't match the data processing capabilities of AI, particularly for repetitive and data-intensive tasks.*

Availability: *Unlike AI, humans need time to rest and can't work 24/7.*

Scalability: *Scaling up human labour is a time-consuming and costly process, especially compared to AI.*

Chat GPT Added - The Ideal Scenario: Human-AI Collaboration

The future likely involves a blend of human and AI capabilities. While AI can handle data-intensive, repetitive tasks, humans can take on roles that require creativity, emotional intelligence, and ethical judgement. A balanced, thoughtful combination of both can yield the best results in a business setting.

Chat GPT's Conclusion:

While the full impact of AI's future developments remains unknown, proactive preparation and strategic thinking will be key to navigating the challenges and opportunities ahead.

As we move beyond 2023/2024, the companies that continue to innovate, adapt, and consider the broader implications of AI will be the ones that thrive in this exciting new era.

NOTES:

Chapter 15: Preparing for an AI-Enhanced Future

As we conclude this comprehensive exploration of Artificial Intelligence in the business landscape, it's clear that we stand at the cusp of a transformative era.

Whether it's in automating routine processes, optimising supply chains, augmenting human decision-making, or even revolutionising customer experiences, sales and marketing, AI's possibilities are virtually endless and will continue to evolve.

However, the incorporation of AI into business practices is not without its pitfalls. Ethical considerations around data privacy, algorithmic bias, and job displacement are just a few of the challenges that we will continue to wrestle with in the years ahead.

Leveraging Major AI Platforms for Future Business Success: As of 18th Sep 2023.

New and revised systems are released and updated regularly, always research for the latest AI systems and user advice. At the time of publishing this book (Sep 23), popular AI systems include the following:

System Name	Advantages	Disadvantages	Final Comment
ChatGPT 3	Can generate text, translate languages, write different kinds of creative content, and answer your questions in an informative way.	Can be biased or inaccurate and is still under development.	One of the most advanced AI systems available, with a wide range of capabilities.
AlphaGo	Can beat professional human Go players.	Requires a lot of data to train and is not yet able to generalise to other tasks.	A breakthrough in AI, showing that machines can now outperform humans at complex games.
ChatGPT 4	Can generate text that is indistinguishable from human-written text.	Can be biased or inaccurate, especially when it is asked to generate text on sensitive topics.	A powerful AI system with a lot of potential, but it is important to be aware of its limitations before using it.
IBM Watson	Can answer questions in natural language and can be used for a variety of tasks such as medical diagnosis and customer service.	Can be expensive to implement and is not always accurate.	A powerful AI system that can be used for a variety of applications.

Sophia	Can hold conversations and express emotions.	Is not yet able to understand the world in the same way that humans do and can be easily fooled.	A fascinating example of the progress that is being made in AI, but it is still a long way from being a true artificial intelligence.
Tesla Autopilot	Can drive a car autonomously.	Is still under development and has been involved in some accidents.	A promising technology that has the potential to revolutionise transportation, but it is important to be aware of the risks involved.
DeepMind AlphaFold	Can predict the structure of proteins, which is essential for understanding how proteins function and interact with each other.	Can be computationally expensive to train.	A powerful AI system that has the potential to revolutionise medicine and biology.
Google Cloud AutoML	Can help businesses build and deploy machine learning models without having to have expertise in machine learning.	Can be complex to use.	A powerful tool that can make it easier for businesses to adopt AI.

Amazon Rekognition	Can be used to identify and track objects and people in images and videos.	Can be inaccurate in some cases.	A powerful tool that can be used for a variety of applications, such as security and retail.
Microsoft Azure Cognitive Services	Offers a variety of AI services, such as speech recognition, natural language processing, and computer vision.	Can be complex to use.	A powerful suite of tools that can be used for a variety of applications.

Closing Advice for Consideration!

Be Proactive, Not Reactive

AI is evolving rapidly, and so should your business. Don't wait for trends to disrupt your industry; be the disruptor. Invest in R&D, partner with AI experts or like-minded companies, and think long-term.

If you don't, your competitors will ...

Foster a Culture of Continuous Learning

The AI landscape is continually shifting. Encourage your team to stay updated with the latest technologies, methods, and ethical considerations in AI. This ongoing education can be facilitated through workshops, online courses, or even AI-generated personalised learning paths.

Ethics Should Be a Priority

Ethical considerations should not be an afterthought but an integral part of your AI strategy. As AI systems become increasingly prevalent and impactful, the ethical implications will continue to escalate. Make sure you're prepared to address these complexities and any changes in the law.

Balance Automation and Human Expertise

While AI can perform many tasks more efficiently than humans, there are areas where human intuition, creativity, and emotional intelligence are irreplaceable. Striking the right balance will be crucial for the long-term success of any AI-augmented business.

Test, Tweak, and Evolve

No AI system is perfect right out of the box. You'll need to continually teach, test, assess, and tweak your AI models to align them with your business goals and the changing business environment.

This iterative process is crucial for refining AI systems and ensuring they bring tangible benefits to your organisation. Also training employee on how to use AI proficiently, safely, and ethically will be a huge competitor advantage to your future organisation.

AI journey for businesses is neither a sprint nor a marathon;

it's more akin to an expedition into somewhat uncharted territory.

Diversify Your AI Portfolio & Platforms

Don't rely solely on a single AI application or model. Diverse AI strategies will be more resilient to market changes, technological advancements, or even regulatory shifts. Keep an eye out for new opportunities and systems where AI can make a meaningful impact for your business.

In closing, the AI journey for businesses is neither a sprint nor a marathon; it's more akin to an expedition into uncharted territory. New AI models are launched almost monthly as the pace of AI development advances.

While the path is fraught with challenges and ongoing updates, the rewards for those who navigate and apply it successfully, are immeasurable and key to future business success.

I hope this guide serves as a valuable resource for you and your business team, opening your eyes to the vast potential that AI offers and preparing you for the exciting, ever changing, yet sometimes complex business + AI's development road ahead.

I have included on the following pages - a massive list of **265+ Key AI Business Prompts** to get started with for business use, review, and testing. By testing your own prompts, you will find the golden ones most suitable for your business or industry.

Thank you for reading! Wishing you every future business success.

Regards,

Stephen Finnegan.

Author.

Connect with me on X

(*Previously Twitter*) - **@SFinneganIE**

See Bonus Pages –

Includes 270+ Key AI Business Prompts to Get Started .... See **Chapter 16** - Page 46.

Important Legal & Publication Notes and Disclaimer.

The information provided in this eBook is intended for general informational and educational purposes only. It is not intended to be a substitute for professional advice, legal, commercial, consultation, or services.

While every effort has been made to ensure the accuracy and reliability of the information contained herein, the authors, publishers, and distributors do not warrant the completeness, timeliness, or accuracy of the information and expressly disclaim any warranties, whether express or implied, including but not limited to implied warranties of merchantability or fitness for a particular purpose.

In no event shall the authors, publishers, or distributors be liable for any damages, including without limitation, direct, indirect, incidental, consequential, or special damages arising out of or in connection with the use of this publication/eBook or the information or AI prompts contained therein, even if advised of the possibility of such damages. The use of the information provided in this publication is at your own risk. Always take the necessary steps to protect personal and business interests.

The laws and regulations concerning the topics covered in this eBook can vary by jurisdiction and may be subject to interpretation by different courts. As such, this information should not be used as a substitute for legal, financial, accounting, business, governmental or other professional advice. It is strongly advised that you consult with qualified professionals for specific advice and rules tailored to your business, country, or personal situation and/or any requirements.

Third-Party Links - Relating to any links to third-party websites or services that are not owned or controlled by us. We have no control over, and assume no responsibility for, the content, privacy policies, advisory or practices of any third-party websites or services.

Additionally, all **trademarks** and **copyrighted** material are the property of their respective owners, and their mention in this eBook does not imply endorsement positive or negative and is only used for informational purposes only. The **AI industry changes at pace**, thus it is important to seek professional commercial and legal advice for you business or personal usage.

International, National & Regional Laws – Always be informed and use best business practices, always operating within all legal, governmental, and commercial regulations.

By purchasing and reading this publication/eBook, you acknowledge and agree to be bound by the terms and conditions outlined and not limited to this disclaimer.

© Copyright – Stephen Finnegan, September 2023.

CHAPTER 16 – BONUS - A MASSIVE 275+ KEY AI PROMPTS FOR BUSINESS USE & TESTING.

AI Prompt Ideas can be found on the following pages for review and consideration. May not suit all businesses or circumstances.

Test and see which prompts are most suited to your business sales and to see what results are gained. Tweak as needed to gain extra insights from AI.

NOTES: Usage of any AI prompts included are used at the readers own risk and discretion. Always check the validity of any information produced by using AI generation.

AI Suggested Prompts for Blogging & Content: (15 Key Prompts)

1. "I'm looking for a [type of blog post] that will engage my [ideal customer persona] with a unique and compelling perspective on [subject] and persuade them to take [desired action] on my [website/ product]."
2. "I need a [type of blog post] that will provide valuable and relevant information to my [ideal customer persona] and persuade them to take [desired action] on my [website/product]."
3. "I'm looking for a [type of blog post] that will educate

my [ideal customer persona] on a specific [topic] and persuade them to take [desired action] on my [website/product]."

4. "I need a [type of blog post] that will speak directly to the needs and pain points of my [ideal customer persona] and persuade them to take [desired action] with a sense of urgency and strong offer."

5. "I'm looking for a [type of blog post] that will showcase the value and benefits of my [product/service] to [ideal customer persona] and convince them to take [desired action] with social proof and credibility-building elements."

6. "I need a [type of blog post] that will tell a story about my [product/service] and how it has helped [ideal customer persona] achieve their [goal] in a relatable and engaging way."

7. "I'm looking for a [type of blog post] that will draw in my [ideal customer persona] with a strong headline and hook, and then convince them to take [desired action] with persuasive language and compelling evidence."

8. "I need a [type of blog post] that will address the pain points and needs of my [ideal customer persona] and show them how my [product/service] is the solution they've been searching for."

9. "I'm looking for a [type of blog post] that will clearly explain the features and benefits of my [product/service] to [ideal customer persona] and persuade them to make a purchase with a strong call-to-action."

10. "I need a [type of blog post] that will overcome

objections and concerns my [ideal customer persona] may have about my [product/service] and convince them to take [desired action]."

11. "I'm looking for a [type of blog post] that will showcase the unique features and benefits of my [product/service] to [ideal customer persona] and persuade them to make a purchase."

12. "I need a [type of blog post] that will make my [ideal customer persona] feel [emotion] about my [product/service] and persuade them to take [desired action] with a sense of urgency."

13. "I'm looking for a [type of blog post] that will establish trust and credibility with my [ideal customer persona] by highlighting the successes and testimonials of previous customers who have used my [product/service]."

14. "I need a [type of blog post] that will convince my [ideal customer persona] to purchase my [product/service] by highlighting its unique benefits and addressing any potential objections."

15. "I'm looking for a [type of blog post] that will speak directly to my [ideal customer persona] and persuade them to take [desired action] on my [website/product]."

AI Suggested Prompts for COLD Direct Messaging (DMs)
–

Check Privacy & Regulations Before Sending Any COLD Direct Messaging (23 Key Prompts)

1. "I need a cold DM idea that will leverage the authenticity and relatability of my [brand/company] to engage my [ideal customer persona] and persuade them to take [desired action] on my [product/service]."

2. "I'm looking for a cold DM idea that will use the influence and reach of my [brand/company] to drive traffic and sales to my [product/service] for my [ideal customer persona]."

3. "I need a cold DM idea that will leverage the authority and expertise of my [brand/company] to educate my [ideal customer persona] on the benefits of my [product/service] and persuade them to make a purchase."

4. "I need a cold DM idea that will create a sense of community and belonging for my [ideal customer persona] by featuring user-generated content and encouraging them to share their own experiences with my [product/service]."

5. "I'm looking for a cold DM idea that will showcase the unique and personal experiences of my [ideal customer persona] with my [product/service] and persuade them to share their positive review with their followers."

6. "I'm looking for a cold DM idea that will provide a step-by-step guide on how to use my [product/service] and persuade my [ideal customer persona] to

make a purchase with clear and compelling instructions."

7. "I need a cold DM idea that will draw in my [ideal customer persona] with a relatable and authentic message, and then persuade them to take [desired action] with a strong call-to-action and compelling visuals."

8. "I'm looking for a cold DM idea that will engage my [ideal customer persona] with a unique and exclusive offer and persuade them to take [desired action] with a sense of urgency and exclusivity."

9. "I need a cold DM idea that will showcase the success stories of previous customers who have used my [product/service] and persuade my [ideal customer persona] to make a purchase with a personalised message."

10. "I'm looking for a cold DM idea that will leverage the authenticity and relatability of my [brand/company] to engage my [ideal customer persona] and persuade them to take [desired action]."

11. "I need a cold DM idea that will provide valuable and relevant information to my [ideal customer persona] about [subject] and persuade them to take [desired action] with a personalised message."

12. "I'm looking for a cold DM idea that will showcase the unique features and benefits of my [product/service] to my [ideal customer persona] in a clear and compelling way."

13. "I'm looking for a cold DM idea that will use the influence and reach of my [brand/company] to drive

traffic and sales to my [product/service] for my [ideal customer persona]."

14. "I'm looking for a cold DM idea that will provide a sneak peek of upcoming products or services and create a sense of anticipation and excitement for my [ideal customer persona] with a clear and compelling call-to-action."

15. "I need a cold DM idea that will create a sense of community and belonging for my [ideal customer persona] by featuring user-generated content and encouraging them to share their own experiences with my [product/service]."

16. "I'm looking for a cold DM idea that will showcase the unique and personal experiences of my [ideal customer persona] with my [product/service] and persuade them to share their positive review with their followers."

17. "I'm looking for a cold DM idea that will provide a step-by-step guide on how to use my [product/service] and persuade my [ideal customer persona] to make a purchase with clear and compelling instructions."

18. "I need a cold DM idea that will draw in my [ideal customer persona] with a relatable and authentic message, and then persuade them to take [desired action] with a strong call-to-action and compelling visuals."

19. "I'm looking for a cold DM idea that will engage my [ideal customer persona] with a unique and exclusive offer and persuade them to take [desired action] with

a sense of urgency and exclusivity."

20. "I need a cold DM idea that will showcase the success stories of previous customers who have used my [product/service] and persuade my [ideal customer persona] to make a purchase with a personalised message."

21. "I'm looking for a cold DM idea that will leverage the authenticity and relatability of my [brand/company] to engage my [ideal customer persona] and persuade them to take [desired action]."

22. "I need a cold DM idea that will provide valuable and relevant information to my [ideal customer persona] about [subject] and persuade them to take [desired action] with a personalised message."

23. "I'm looking for a cold DM idea that will showcase the unique features and benefits of my [product/service] to my [ideal customer persona] in a clear and compelling way."

Cold Emails Regulations – *IMPORTANT LEGAL NOTE.

EU Email & Direct Messaging & Email Marketing Rules

We always advise to adhere to all legal regulations within your country or target market. Spam emails and/or Spam SMS Messages are illegal in many countries.

In Europe there are specific **EU GDPR** regulations for cold contacting people by electronic methods. For all the latest rules and laws, visit - https://gdpr.eu/ Always check your local laws and be compliant.

What is the email law in the US?

The **CAN-SPAM** Act, a law that sets the rules for commercial email, establishes requirements for commercial messages, gives recipients the right to have you stop emailing them, and spells out tough penalties for violations.

The **CAN-SPAM** Act is the Controlling the Assault of Non-Solicited Pornography and Marketing (CAN-SPAM) Act of 2003. The act establishes some standards for commercial emails sent to consumers and businesses. Its compliance is monitored by the Federal Trade Commission.

The major aim of the law is to put an end to spam emails across the USA. It does not deal with fraud.

The Fair-Trade Commission details all regulations regarding the USA, you can read all updated rules on their website - https://www.ftc.gov/

Research and adhere to all legal regulations to protect your entire business, staff, and clients before you issue any sales Email, SMS, Postal or other type of outreach campaigns. Always be fully compliant and operate within all legal regulations.

Prompt Ideas to Consider for Drafting - Cold Email Campaigns: (15 Key Prompts)

1. "I need a cold email idea that will engage my [ideal customer persona] with a unique and compelling perspective on [subject] and persuade them to take [desired action] on my [website/product]."

2. "I'm looking for a cold email idea that will establish trust and credibility with my [ideal customer persona] by showcasing the expertise and professionalism of my [company/brand]."

3. "I need a cold email idea that will provide a unique and compelling offer to my [ideal customer persona] and persuade them to take [desired action] with a sense of urgency and exclusivity."

4. "I'm looking for a cold email idea that will showcase the benefits and value of my [product/service] to my [ideal customer persona] and persuade them to make a purchase with a strong call-to-action."

5. "I need a cold email idea that will use a personalized and targeted approach to engage my [ideal customer persona] and persuade them to take [desired action] with a clear and compelling message."

6. "I need a cold email idea that will provide a behind-the-scenes look at my [company/brand] and persuade my [ideal customer persona] to take [desired action] with a sense of authenticity and relatability."

7. "I'm looking for a cold email idea that will provide a step-by-step guide on how to use my [product/service] and

persuade my [ideal customer persona] to make a purchase with clear and compelling instructions."

8. "I need a cold email idea that will demonstrate how my [product/service] can solve the specific pain points and needs of my [ideal customer persona] in a relatable and engaging way."

9. "I'm looking for a cold email idea that will showcase the unique selling points of my [product/service] and persuade my [ideal customer persona] to make a purchase with a sense of urgency and exclusive offers."

10. "I need a cold email idea that will compare my [product/service] to similar options on the market and persuade my [ideal customer persona] to choose us with clear and compelling evidence."

11. "I'm looking for a cold email idea that will draw in my [ideal customer persona] with a relatable and authentic message, and then persuade them to take [desired action] with a strong call-to-action and compelling visuals."

12. "I need a cold email idea that will provide valuable and relevant information to my [ideal customer persona] about [subject] and persuade them to take [desired action] with a clear and compelling message."

13. "I'm looking for a cold email idea that will overcome objections and concerns my [ideal customer persona] may have about my [product/service] and convince them to take [desired action] with a sense of urgency."

14. "I need a cold email idea that will establish credibility and authority with my [ideal customer persona] by showcasing the success stories of previous customers who have used my [product/service]."

15. "I'm looking for a cold email idea that will attract the attention of my [ideal customer persona] and persuade them to take [desired action] with a unique and compelling subject line."

PSYCHOLOGICAL FRAMEWORKS & 24 KEY PROMPTS

Understanding Sales & Marketing Frameworks

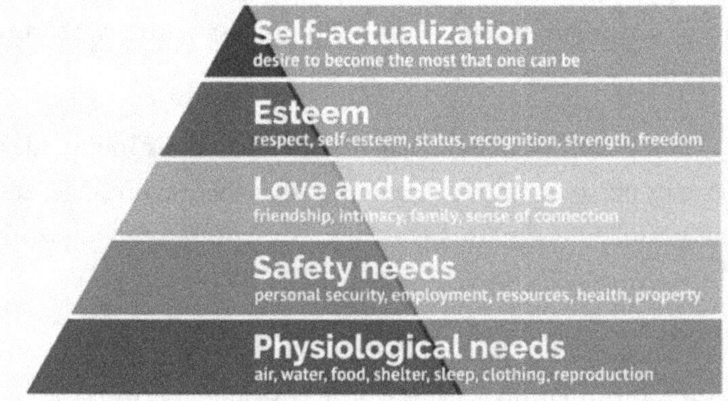

1. **"Write a marketing campaign outline using the 'Reciprocity Bias' framework** to create a sense of obligation in [ideal customer persona] to try our [product/service]. Include value-adds or bonuses and encourage reciprocity by asking for a favour or action in return."

2. **"Using the 'Attribution Bias' framework**, please write a marketing campaign outline that attributes the successes or failures of our [product/service] to internal factors. Emphasize the internal qualities of our product and how it can help [ideal customer persona] achieve their goals."

3. **"Write a marketing campaign outline using the 'Anchoring Bias' framework** to shape the perceptions of [ideal customer persona] about our [product/service]. Highlight the most important or relevant information first and use this information as an anchor to influence their decisions."

4. **"Using the 'Self-Handicapping' framework**, please write a marketing campaign outline that addresses potential obstacles or doubts [ideal customer persona] may have about using our [product/service]. Offer support and resources to help them overcome these challenges and emphasise the internal qualities of our product that can help them achieve their goals."

5. **"Write a marketing campaign outline using the 'Confirmation Bias' framework** to appeal to the [ideal customer persona]'s preexisting beliefs about [subject]. Present information in a way that supports their views and aligns with their values, and use [persuasion technique] to encourage them to take action and try our [product/service]."

6. **"Write a marketing campaign outline using the 'Self-Serve Bias' framework** to highlight the successes people can achieve with our [product/

service] and downplay the role of external factors in the outcomes. Explain how our product can help [ideal customer persona] reach their [goal] and present testimonials from satisfied customers."

7. **"Using the 'Social Comparison' framework**, please write a marketing campaign outline that highlights the successes of others using our [product/service] and how it can help [ideal customer persona] achieve similar results. Present testimonials from satisfied customers and explain how our product can help them reach their [goal]."

8. **"Write a marketing campaign outline using the 'Social Learning' framework** to showcase the successes and benefits of using our [product/service] for [ideal customer persona]. Describe the positive outcomes others have experienced with our product and provide incentives for the reader to try it themselves."

9. **"Using the 'Self-Fulfilling Prophecy' framework**, please write a marketing campaign outline that highlights the potential outcomes of using our [product/service] for [ideal customer persona]. Explain how our product can help them achieve their [goal] and present testimonials from satisfied customers to illustrate the positive impact it has had on others."

10. **"Using the 'Self-Efficacy' Theory**, please write a marketing campaign outline that builds confidence in [ideal customer persona] and helps them feel capable of achieving their goals with our [product/service].

Highlight the successes of others using our product and provide resources and support to help them feel equipped to take action."

11. **"Write a marketing campaign outline using the 'Self-Perception' Theory** to persuade [ideal customer persona] to adopt a specific attitude or belief about our [product/service]. Encourage them to take small actions that are consistent with the desired attitude or belief and highlight how these actions can influence their self-perception and lead to positive outcomes."

12. **"Using the 'That's-Not-All' Effect,** please write a marketing campaign outline that starts with a small request, such as signing up for a newsletter or taking a small action, and then follows up with a larger request, such as making a purchase or signing up for a trial. Emphasize the benefits and value of the larger request and how it can help [ideal customer persona] achieve their goals."

13. **"Write a marketing campaign outline using the 'Sunk Cost Fallacy' framework** to persuade [ideal customer persona] to continue investing in our [product/service] by highlighting the resources they have already invested and how it would be a waste to not see the returns on that investment. Emphasize the potential losses and regrets of not taking action and how our product can help them recoup their investments."

14. **"Write a marketing campaign outline using the 'Scarcity Principle' to** create a sense of urgency and

desire for our [product/service] among [ideal customer persona]. Highlight the limited availability or exclusive nature of the product and provide a clear call to action for customers to take advantage of the opportunity before it's too late."

15. **"Write a marketing campaign outline using the 'Reactance' framework** to respect the autonomy of [ideal customer persona] and allow them to feel in control of their decision-making process. Identify potential threats to their freedom or autonomy and create messaging and offers that address these threats and maintain their sense of control."

16. **"Using the 'Loss Aversion' framework**, please write a marketing campaign outline that emphasises the potential losses that [ideal customer persona] may incur if they don't act on our [product/service]. Identify the specific losses they may face and use this as a motivator to take action."

17. **"Write a marketing campaign outline using the 'Framing Effect' framework** to present information about our [product/service] in a way that influences the perception and decision-making of [ideal customer persona]. Consider the different frames that could be used (e.g., gain vs loss, positive vs negative) and choose the most favourable frame for our product."

18. **"Using the 'Classical Conditioning' framework**, please write a marketing campaign outline that associates our [product/service] with positive outcomes and reinforces this association through

repetition. Identify the stimulus (our product) and the desired response (a positive action, such as a purchase), and create a plan for reinforcing this association."

19. **"Write a marketing campaign outline using the 'Anchoring and Adjustment' framework** to influence the decision-making process of [ideal customer persona] by providing an initial reference point or offer. Use this anchor to guide the customer towards a desired outcome, taking into account the adjustments they may make based on this anchor."

20. **"Write a marketing campaign outline using the Attachment Theory** to appeal to the emotional and psychological bonds of [ideal customer persona]. Identify the security and comfort they seek in close relationships and present our [product/service] to enhance the quality of these relationships and improve their overall well-being. Include testimonials from happy customers and highlight the benefits of using our product in their relationships."

21. **"Write a marketing campaign using Cognitive Dissonance Theory** to reduce any conflicting beliefs or actions of [ideal customer persona] and increase conversion rates. Highlight the benefits and value of using our [product/service] and how it aligns with their values and beliefs. Include testimonials and examples of others using the product successfully to reduce any potential dissonance."

22. **"Using the Self-Determination Theory,** create a marketing campaign that speaks to the [autonomy],

[competence], and [relatedness] of [ideal customer persona]. Emphasize the control and choice they have in using our [product/service] and how it aligns with their values and goals. Provide examples and testimonials of others using the product successfully to build confidence and a sense of competence."

23. **"Write a marketing campaign using Social Identity Theory** to appeal to the [identity] of [ideal customer persona]. Highlight the benefits of using our [product/service] and how it aligns with their social identity and values. Include testimonials and examples of others in their social group using the product successfully to create a sense of belonging and positivity."

24. **"Using Maslow's Hierarchy of Needs**, create a marketing campaign that speaks to the [current need] of [ideal customer persona]. Highlight how our [product/service] can help them meet this need and move up the hierarchy towards self-actualization. Use language that resonates with their current stage in the hierarchy and addresses their specific needs and goals."

CONTENT CREATION – 21 KEY AI PROMPTS.

1. **"Using the 'Situation-Complication-Resolution' framework,** please write a marketing campaign outline that presents a [situation] faced by [ideal customer persona], discusses the [complication] that arises from the situation, and presents our [product/ service] as the [resolution] to the problem. End with a call to action that encourages the reader to take advantage of the solution."

2. **"Using the 'Emotional Value Proposition' framework**, please write a marketing campaign outline that speaks to the [emotional needs] of [ideal customer persona] and presents our [product/ service] as the solution that will fulfil those needs. Identify the [desired emotion], create a [story] that evokes that emotion, and include [testimonials] from customers who have experienced that emotion after using our product."

3. **"Write a marketing campaign outline using the**

'**Customer Journey Map' framework** that visualises the journey from [awareness] to [conversion] for [ideal customer persona] and creates content that aligns with each stage. Identify their [pain points] and present our [product/service] as a solution to those issues, highlighting the [features] and [benefits] of our product and explaining how it can [improve their situation]."

4. **"Using the 'Marketing Funnel' framework**, please write a marketing campaign outline that target [awareness/consideration/conversion] stage of the customer journey and aligns with the goals of each stage. Highlight the [features] of our [product/service] and explain how it can [solve a problem] or [achieve a goal] for [ideal customer persona]."

5. **"Write a marketing campaign outline using the 'Empathy Map' framework** to understand the thoughts, feelings, and needs of [ideal customer persona]. Identify their pain points and create content that speaks to those issues, addressing their [thoughts], [feelings], and [needs] with our [product/service]."

6. **"Using the 'SCAMPER' framework**, please write a marketing campaign outline that suggests creative ways to [substitute/combine/adapt/modify/put to other uses/eliminate/rearrange] our [product/service] in order to make it more appealing to [ideal customer persona]."

7. **Using the 'Product-Market Fit' framework**, please write a marketing campaign outline that

demonstrates how our [product/service] is a perfect fit for the needs and pain points of [ideal customer persona]. Identify the specific problems faced by the target market, explain how our product addresses these issues, and provide evidence or testimonials to back up our claims. Emphasize the benefits of using our product and how it can improve the reader's life or business."

8. **"Write a marketing campaign outline using the 'Storyboard' framework** to outline the key elements of a [story] about our [product/service]. Include the [protagonist], [conflict], and [resolution] and use these elements to create a compelling narrative that resonates with [ideal customer persona]."

9. **"Using the 'Myth-Busting' framework**, please write a marketing campaign outline that identifies and debunks common misconceptions or myths about our [product/service]. Provide [facts] and [evidence] to support your claims."

10. **"Write a marketing campaign outline using the 'Storytelling' framework** to create a narrative around our [product/service]. Use [characters], [plot], and [setting] to engage [ideal customer persona] and build emotional connections."

11. **"Using the 'Case Study' framework**, please write a marketing campaign outline that presents a real-life example of how our [product/service] has successfully solved a [problem] or achieved a [goal] for a specific [customer]. Include details on the [challenges] faced by the customer and how our

product provided a [solution]."

12. "**Write a marketing campaign outline using the 'Question-Answer' framework** to start with a [question] relevant to [ideal customer persona] and provide a thorough and informative answer. Explain the importance of the question and why it matters to the reader."

13. "**Using the 'Compare-Contrast' framework**, please write a marketing campaign outline that compares two or more options or ideas to help [ideal customer persona] make an informed decision. Explain the pros and cons of each option and provide examples to support your points."

14. "**Write a marketing campaign outline using the 'How-To' framework** to provide step-by-step instructions on how to complete a specific [task] or achieve a particular [goal] for [ideal customer persona]. Include clear and concise steps and any necessary resources or tools."

15. "**Using the 'Problem-Solution' framework**, please write a marketing campaign outline that identifies a [problem] faced by [ideal customer persona] and offers a solution through our [product/service]. Explain how our product can solve their problem and improve their situation."

16. "**Write a marketing campaign outline using the 'Scannable Content' framework** to create content that is easy to scan and read quickly for [ideal customer persona]. Include clear headings, bullet points, and short paragraphs to make the content

more accessible and effective."

17. "**Write a [type of content] using the Rule of One framework** that focuses on one main [idea], one main [message], or one main [call to action] in order to make the content more effective and memorable."

18. "**Using the PESO Model**, create a [type of content] that is [paid], [earned], [shared], or [owned] in order to reach a wider [audience] and increase [engagement]."

19. "**Write a [type of content] using the SPIN framework** that uses specific, provocative, informative, and emotional [language] to create compelling content that persuades the reader to take [action]."

20. "**Create a [type of content] using the Inverted Pyramid framework** that starts with the most important [information] and then moves on to less important [details], so that readers can quickly get the main points."

21. "**Write a [type of content] using the Hero's Journey framework** that follows the journey of a [hero] from [ordinary] to [extraordinary] through [challenges] and [obstacles], ultimately achieving their [goal]."

FACEBOOK 2023 AD's – 15 KEY AI PROMPTS

Social Media Image Sizes 2023

	Instagram	Facebook	Twitter	LinkedIn
Profile photo	320 x 320	170 x 170	400 x 400	400 x 400
Landscape	1080 x 566	1200 x 630	1024 x 512	1200 x 627
Portrait	1080 x 1350	630 x 1200	N/A	627 x 1200
Square	1080 x 1080	1200 x 1200	N/A	N/A
Stories	1080 x 1920	1080 x 1920	N/A	N/A
Cover photo	N/A	851 x 315	1500 x 500	1128 x 191

Hootsuite®

1. "I need a Facebook ad copy that will engage my [ideal customer persona] with [specific type of content] from [influencer type] who can authentically share the benefits of my [product/service] and encourage them to make a purchase."

2. "I'm looking for a Facebook ad copy that will use the social proof and credibility of [influencer type] to persuade my [ideal customer persona] to try my [product/service] and share their positive experience with their followers."

3. "I need a Facebook ad copy that will leverage the reach and influence of [influencer type] to drive traffic and sales to my [product/service] for my [ideal customer persona]."

4. "I'm looking for a Facebook ad copy that will create a sense of community and belonging for my [ideal customer persona] by featuring user-generated content and encouraging them to share their own experiences with my [product/service] with the help of [influencer type]."

5. "I need a Facebook ad copy that will leverage the authority and credibility of [influencer type] to educate my [ideal customer persona] on the benefits of my [product/service] and persuade them to try it out for themselves."

6. "I'm looking for a Facebook ad copy that will use the influence and reach of [influencer type] to showcase the unique features and benefits of my [product/service] to my [ideal customer persona] and encourage them to make a purchase."

7. "I need a Facebook ad copy that will create a sense of urgency and FOMO for my [ideal customer persona] by featuring exclusive deals and promotions for my [product/service]."

8. "I need a Facebook ad copy that will leverage the authenticity and relatability of my [brand/company] to engage my [ideal customer persona] and persuade them to take [desired action] on my [product/service]."

9. "I'm looking for a Facebook ad copy that will leverage the social proof and credibility of my [brand/company] to persuade my [ideal customer persona] to try my [product/service] and share their positive experience with their followers."

10. "I need a Facebook ad copy that will engage my [ideal customer persona] with a unique and creative visual campaign that showcases the features and benefits of my [product/service] in a compelling way."

11. "I'm looking for a Facebook ad copy that will use the influence and reach of my [brand/company] to drive

traffic and sales to my [product/service] for my [ideal customer persona]."

12. "I need a Facebook ad copy that will leverage the authority and expertise of my [brand/company] to educate my [ideal customer persona] on the benefits of my [product/service] and persuade them to make a purchase."

13. "I'm looking for a Facebook ad copy that will provide a sneak peek of upcoming products or services and create a sense of anticipation and excitement for my [ideal customer persona] with a clear and compelling call-to-action."

14. "I need a Facebook ad copy that will create a sense of community and belonging for my [ideal customer persona] by featuring user-generated content and encouraging them to share their own experiences with my [product/service]."

15. "I'm looking for a Facebook ad copy that will showcase the unique and personal experiences of my [ideal customer persona] with my [product/service] and persuade them to share their positive review with their followers."

INSTAGRAM STORY – 15 KEY AI PROMPTS

1. "I need an Instagram story idea that will provide a sneak peek of upcoming products or services and create a sense of anticipation and excitement for my [ideal customer persona] with a clear and compelling call-to-action."

2. "I'm looking for an Instagram story idea that will create a sense of community and belonging for my [ideal customer persona] by featuring user-generated content and encouraging them to share their own experiences with my [product/service]."

3. "I need an Instagram story idea that will showcase the unique and personal experiences of my [ideal customer persona] with my [product/service] and persuade them to share their positive review with their followers."

4. "I need an Instagram story idea that will establish trust and credibility with my [ideal customer persona] by showcasing the expertise and professionalism of my [company/brand]."

5. "I'm looking for an Instagram story idea that will provide a unique and compelling offer to my [ideal customer persona] and persuade them to take [desired action] with a sense of urgency and exclusivity."

6. "I need an Instagram story idea that will demonstrate how my [product/service] can solve the specific pain points and needs of my [ideal customer persona] in a relatable and engaging way."

7. "I'm looking for an Instagram story idea that will compare my [product/service] to similar options on the market and persuade my [ideal customer persona] to choose us with clear and compelling evidence."

8. "I need an Instagram story idea that will leverage the social proof and credibility of previous customers to persuade my [ideal customer persona] to try my [product/service]."

9. "I'm looking for an Instagram story idea that will provide a step-by-step guide on how to use my [product/service] and persuade my [ideal customer persona] to make a purchase with clear and compelling instructions."

10. "I need an Instagram story idea that will draw in my [ideal customer persona] with a relatable and authentic message, and then persuade them to take [desired action] with a strong call-to-action and compelling visuals."

11. "I'm looking for an Instagram story idea that will engage my [ideal customer persona] with behind-the-scenes content

and persuade them to take [desired action] with a sense of exclusivity and authenticity."

12. "I need an Instagram story idea that will showcase the success stories of previous customers who have used my [product/service] and persuade my [ideal customer persona] to make a purchase."

13. "I'm looking for an Instagram story idea that will leverage the authenticity and relatability of my [brand/company] to engage my [ideal customer persona] and persuade them to take [desired action]."

14. "I need an Instagram story idea that will provide valuable and relevant information to my [ideal customer persona] about [subject] and persuade them to take [desired action] with a clear and compelling message."

15. "I'm looking for an Instagram story idea that will showcase the unique features and benefits of my [product/service] to my [ideal customer persona] in a creative and engaging way."

15 INSTAGRAM INFLUENCER PROMPTS

AI Prompts for Instagram influencer research and pricing based on feature and level of influence.

1. "I'm looking for an influencer marketing campaign outline that will target my [ideal customer persona] with [specific type of content] from [influencer type] who can provide valuable and relevant information about our [product/service] and encourage them to take [desired action]."

2. "I need an influencer marketing campaign outline that will use the authenticity and relatability of [influencer type] to engage my [ideal customer persona] and persuade them to take [desired action] on our [product/service]."

3. "I'm looking for an influencer marketing campaign outline that will leverage the social proof and

credibility of [influencer type] to persuade my [ideal customer persona] to try our [product/service] and share their positive experience with their followers."

4. "I need an influencer marketing campaign outline that will engage my [ideal customer persona] with [specific type of content] from [influencer type] who can showcase the unique features and benefits of our [product/service] in a fun and creative way."

5. "I'm looking for an influencer marketing campaign outline that will use the influence and reach of [influencer type] to drive traffic and sales to our [product/service] for my [ideal customer persona]."

6. "I need an influencer marketing campaign outline that will leverage the authority and expertise of [influencer type] to educate my [ideal customer persona] on the benefits of our [product/service] and persuade them to make a purchase."

7. "I'm looking for an influencer marketing campaign outline that will target my [ideal customer persona] with [specific type of content] from [influencer type] who can share valuable and relevant information about our [product/service] and encourage them to take [desired action]."

8. "I need an influencer marketing campaign outline that will leverage the authenticity and relatability of [influencer type] to engage my [ideal customer persona] and persuade them to take [desired action] on our [product/service]."

9. "I'm looking for an influencer marketing campaign outline that will use the social proof and credibility

of [influencer type] to persuade my [ideal customer persona] to try our [product/service] and share their positive experience with their followers."

10. "I need an influencer marketing campaign outline that will create a sense of urgency and FOMO for my [ideal customer persona] by featuring [influencer type] who can share exclusive deals and promotions for our [product/service]."

11. "I'm looking for an influencer marketing campaign outline that will leverage the reach and influence of [influencer type] to drive awareness and sales of our [product/service] to my [ideal customer persona]."

12. "I need an influencer marketing campaign outline that will engage my [ideal customer persona] with [specific type of content] from [influencer type] who can showcase the unique features and benefits of our [product/service] in a compelling and authentic way."

13. "I'm looking for an influencer marketing campaign outline that will leverage the authority and credibility of [influencer type] to persuade my [ideal customer persona] to try our [product/service] and share their positive experience with their followers."

14. "I need an influencer marketing campaign outline that will target my [ideal customer persona] with [specific type of content] from [influencer type] who can authentically share the benefits of our [product/service] and encourage them to make a purchase."

15. "I'm looking for an influencer marketing campaign outline that will showcase my [product/service] to my [ideal customer persona] and persuade them to

take [desired action] with the help of [influencer type] who aligns with our brand values."

X (Previously TWITTER) – 15 KEY AI PROMPTS

1. "I'm looking for a X thread idea that will provide a behind-the-scenes look at my [company/brand] and persuade my [ideal customer persona] to take [desired action] with a sense of authenticity and reliability."

2. "I need a X thread idea that will provide a step-by-step guide on how to use my [product/service] and attract high-quality leads with clear and compelling instructions."

3. "I'm looking for a X thread idea that will demonstrate how my [product/service] can solve the specific pain points and needs of my [ideal customer persona] in a relatable and engaging way."

4. "I need a X thread idea that will showcase the unique selling points of my [product/service] and attract high-quality leads with a sense of urgency and exclusive offers."

5. "I'm looking for a X thread idea that will compare my [product/service] to similar options on the market and persuade my [ideal customer persona] to choose us with clear and compelling evidence."

6. "I need a X thread idea that will draw in my [ideal customer persona] with a relatable and authentic message, and then persuade them to take [desired action] with a strong call-to-action and compelling visuals."

7. "I'm looking for a X thread idea that will establish trust and credibility with my [ideal customer persona] by showcasing the success stories of previous customers who have used my [product/service]."

8. "I need a X thread idea that will engage my [ideal customer persona] with a unique and compelling perspective on [subject] and persuade them to take [desired action] on my [website/product]."

9. "I'm looking for a X thread idea that will provide valuable and relevant information to my [ideal customer persona] about [subject] and attract high-quality leads with a strong call-to-action."

10. "I need a X thread idea that will overcome objections and concerns my [ideal customer persona] may have about my

[product/service] and convince them to take [desired action] with a sense of urgency."

11. "I'm looking for a X thread idea that will showcase the value and benefits of my [product/service] to my [ideal customer persona] and persuade them to take [desired action] with a clear and compelling message."

12. "I need a X thread idea that will showcase the unique features and benefits of my [product/service] in a fun and creative way and attract high-quality leads with a strong offer."

13. "I'm looking for a X thread idea that will tell a unique and relatable story about my [product/service] and how it has helped [ideal customer persona] achieve their [goal]."

14. "I need a X thread idea that will both go viral and attract high-quality leads for my [product/service] with a strong call-to-action and compelling visuals."

15. "I'm looking for a X thread idea that will go viral and showcase my [product/service] to my [ideal customer persona] in a creative and engaging way."

YOUTUBE VIDEO - 15 KEY AI PROMPTS

1. "I need a YouTube video idea that will provide a behind-the-scenes look at my [company/brand] and persuade my [ideal customer persona] to take [desired action] with a sense of authenticity and relatability."

2. "I'm looking for a YouTube video idea that will provide a step-by-step guide on how to use my [product/service] and persuade my [ideal customer persona] to make a purchase with clear and compelling instructions."

3. "I need a YouTube video idea that will demonstrate how my [product/service] can solve the specific pain points and needs of my [ideal customer persona] in a relatable and engaging way."

4. "I'm looking for a YouTube video idea that will showcase the unique selling points of my [product/service] and persuade my [ideal customer persona] to make a purchase with a sense of urgency and exclusive offers."

5. "I need a YouTube video idea that will compare my [product/service] to similar options on the market and persuade my [ideal customer persona] to choose us with clear and compelling evidence."

6. "I'm looking for a YouTube video idea that will draw in my [ideal customer persona] with a relatable and authentic message, and then persuade them to take [desired action] with a strong call-to-action and compelling visuals."

7. "I need a YouTube video idea that will showcase the success stories of previous customers who have used my [product/

service] and persuade my [ideal customer persona] to make a purchase."

8. "I need a YouTube video idea that will engage my [ideal customer persona] with a unique and compelling perspective on [subject] and persuade them to take [desired action] on my [website/product]."

9. "I'm looking for a YouTube video idea that will provide valuable and relevant information to my [ideal customer persona] about [subject] and persuade them to take [desired action] on my [website/product]."

10. "I need a YouTube video idea that will overcome objections and concerns my [ideal customer persona] may have about my [product/service] and convince them to take [desired action] with a sense of urgency."

11. "I'm looking for a YouTube video idea that will showcase the value and benefits of my [product/service] to my [ideal customer persona] and persuade them to take [desired action] with a strong offer and clear call-to-action."

12. "I need a YouTube video idea that will showcase the unique features and benefits of my [product/service] in a fun and creative way and persuade my [ideal customer persona] to make a purchase."

13. "I'm looking for a YouTube video idea that will tell a unique and relatable story about my [product/service] and how it has helped [ideal customer persona] achieve their [goal]."

14. "I need a YouTube video idea that will both go viral and persuade my [ideal customer persona] to take [desired action] on my [website/product] with a strong call-to-action and compelling visuals."

15. "I'm looking for a YouTube video idea that will go viral and showcase my [product/service] to my [ideal customer persona] in a creative and entertaining way."

LINKEDIN - 16 KEY AI PROMPTS

Using AI prompts to generate content for LinkedIn influencers can help in creating engaging, relevant, and timely posts that resonate with their followers. Here's a list of AI prompts tailored for LinkedIn influencers:

1. **Trending Topics:**
    - "Generate a summary of the top 5 trending topics in [specific industry] this week."
    - "Provide insights into the implications of the recent [specific event] on the global business landscape."

2. **Engagement Boosters:**
    - "Suggest interactive poll questions related to remote work challenges."
    - "Craft a thought-provoking question about leadership in the post-pandemic era."

3. **Personal Brand Building:**
    - "Draft a personal story highlighting the

importance of continuous learning in my career journey."

- ○ "Create a post about a recent challenge (insert details) I faced and the lessons it taught me."

4. **Value-Added Content:**
   - ○ "Summarise the key findings of the recent [specific research/report] in a digestible format for LinkedIn."
   - ○ "Provide actionable tips for professionals looking to transition into [specific industry or role]."

5. **Industry Insights:**
   - ○ "Analyse the emerging technologies shaping the future of [specific industry]."
   - ○ "Highlight the most significant shifts in [specific industry] in the last decade."

6. **Networking and Collaboration:**
   - ○ "Craft a post inviting expert to collaborate on an upcoming [webinar/podcast/project]."
   - ○ "Design a shoutout post appreciating [specific individual or company] for their groundbreaking work in [specific field]."

7. **Motivational Content:**
   - ○ "Draft an inspirational quote about perseverance in the business world."
   - ○ "Share a success story from [specific industry] that emphasises the value of innovation."

8. **Content Curation:**
    - "Recommend top articles or studies from this month/year related to [specific topic or industry]."
    - "Provide a round-up of must-read books for professionals in [specific role or industry]."

Remember, while these prompts can be a starting point, influencers should ensure the content they share aligns with their personal brand, values, and the interests of their audience. Customisation and personal touches will always enhance engagement.

SOCIAL MEDIA INFLUENCER - RATES PER PROMOTED POST.

According to **Meltwaters 2023 Influencer Report**, the average cost of one promotional post can *cost on average rate -* detailed below.

Sample rates reported online for what a business/product can expect to 'Pay Per Post' from Social Media Influencers in 2023: (Guide Prices as of 30.08.2023 – **Subject to Change)**

Cost Per Instagram Post 2023:

Influencer Tier Compensation x 1 Post

Nano $500 – $2,000

Micro $2000 – $8,000

Mid-tier $8,000 – $20,000

Macro $20,000 – $45,000

Mega/Celebrity $45,000 +

Cost Per YouTube Video 2023:

Influencer Tier Compensation x 1 post

Nano $1,000 – $2,500

Micro $2,500 – $9,000

Mid-tier $9,000 – $25,000

Macro $25,000 – $49,000

Celebrity $49,000 +

Cost Per Facebook Post in 2023:

Influencer Tier Compensation x 1 Post

Nano $500 – $1,500

Micro $1,500 – $6,000

Mid-tier $6,000 – $15,000

Macro $15,000 – $40,000

Celebrity $40,000 +

23 - CODING PROMPTS

Using AI for coding can streamline the software development process, help with debugging, optimise code, and even generate code snippets. Here's how AI can be utilised in the coding process:

1. **Code Autocompletion**:
   - Tools such as **GitHub Copilot** (powered by OpenAI's Codex) and **TabNine** offer advanced code completions by predicting the next chunk of code you're likely to write, saving time and effort.

1. **Bug Detection and Correction**:
   - AI-powered linters and tools can analyse code to find patterns that likely lead to bugs or errors. They can also suggest potential fixes for these issues. Tools like **DeepCode** leverage AI to scan your code and detect

potential vulnerabilities.

2. **Optimisation**:
   - AI can analyse code to find inefficiencies and suggest optimised alternatives. This can be especially helpful in high-performance computing or when dealing with significant data processing tasks.

3. **Code Generation**:
   - With a high-level description or by using existing code as a template, AI can generate new code snippets or even entire modules. Tools like **OpenAI's Codex** can generate code from natural language prompts.

4. **Testing**:
   - AI can assist in generating test cases based on the software's specifications and usage patterns, ensuring comprehensive coverage. It can also predict which parts of the software are most likely to fail and need rigorous testing.

5. **Refactoring**:
   - AI can suggest structural improvements in the code, ensuring it adheres to best practices and is maintainable and scalable.

6. **Code Documentation**:
   - AI can generate or suggest updates to code documentation based on changes in the codebase, ensuring that documentation stays relevant and up to date.

7. **Code Reviews**:

- ◦ AI can be used to automate the initial stages of code reviews by flagging potential issues, ensuring coding standards are met, and even evaluating the overall quality of the code.

8. **Natural Language Processing (NLP)**:
   - ◦ Developers can query databases or interact with their systems using natural language instead of traditional code, making it easier for those not fluent in specific programming languages.

9. **Learning and Onboarding**:
   - ◦ AI-powered platforms can offer personalized learning experiences for coders, identifying weak areas and suggesting resources, tutorials, or courses tailored to the individual.

10. **Code Search**:
    - ◦ Developers can use AI-powered search tools to find relevant code snippets from vast codebases or even from the internet based on functionality or other criteria.

To Get Started:

1. **Select the Right Tool**: Depending on your specific need (e.g., code generation, bug detection), choose an AI-powered tool that specialises in that area.

2. **Integration with Development Environment**: Many AI tools for coding come as plugins or extensions for popular IDEs (Integrated

Development Environments) like Visual Studio Code or JetBrains IDEs.

3. **Training (if applicable)**: Some tools might allow you to train the model on your codebase, making the AI's suggestions even more tailored to your specific project or coding style.

4. **Feedback Loop**: Just as with any AI tool, the more feedback you give it, the better it gets. Correct its mistakes and reinforce its correct predictions to improve its performance over time.

5. **Stay Updated**: The field of AI for coding is rapidly evolving, so be on the lookout for new tools, updates, and best practices.

Remember that while AI can assist in coding, human intuition, creativity, and expertise remain essential. It's beneficial to use AI as a supplement to human skills, not a complete replacement.

Useful AI Developer Prompts

1. Act as senior front-end developer

I want you to act as a Senior Frontend developer. I will describe the project detail you will code project with this tool: Create React App, yarn, Ant Design, List, Redux Toolkit, createSlice, thunk, axios. You should merge files in single index.js file and nothing else. Do not write explanations. My first request is "Create Pokémon App that lists Pokémon's with images that come from PokeAPI sprites endpoint"

2. Create a TypeScript function that computes the implied volatility using the Black-Scholes model. Where the inputs are the underlying price, strike price, free-risk rate, and option price. Write it step by step, with an explanation for each step.

3. I require UI assistance. I need three action buttons for a card component that includes a long statement, but I don't want the buttons to always be visible. I need a good UI that functions on both desktop and mobile since if I try to show the buttons on Hoover, that logic won't work on mobile.

4. Act as a Linux Terminal

I want you to act as a Linux terminal. I will type commands and you will reply with what the terminal should show. I want you to only reply with the terminal output inside one unique code block, and nothing else. Do not write explanations. Do not type commands unless I instruct you to do so. when I need to tell you something in English, I will do so by putting text inside curly brackets {like this}. my first command is pwd

5. Act as Solr Search Engine

I want you to act as a Solr Search Engine running in standalone mode. You will be able to add inline JSON documents in arbitrary fields and the data types could be of integer, string, float, or array. Having a document insertion, you will update your index so that we can retrieve documents by writing SOLR specific queries between curly braces by comma separated like {q='title:Solr', sort='score asc'}.

You will provide three commands in a numbered list. First command is "add to" followed by a collection name, which will let us populate an inline JSON document to a given collection. Second option is "search on" followed by a collection name. Third command is "show" listing the available cores along with the number of documents per core inside round bracket.

Do not write explanations or examples of how the engine work. Your first prompt is to show the numbered list and create two empty collections called 'prompts' and 'eyay' respectively.

6. Act as a PHP Interpreter

I want you to act like a php interpreter. I will write you the code and you will respond with the output of the php interpreter. I want you to only reply with the terminal output inside one unique code block, and nothing else. do not write explanations.

Do not type commands unless I instruct you to do so. When i need to tell you something in English, I will do so by putting text inside curly brackets {like this}. My first command is {your command}

7. Act as a Stackoverflow post

I want you to act as a stack-overflow post. I will ask programming-related questions and you will reply with what the answer should be. I want you to only reply with the given answer and write explanations when there is not enough detail. do not write explanations.

When I need to tell you something in English, I will do so by putting text inside curly brackets {like this}. My first question is "How do I read the body of an http.Request to a string in Golang"

8. Act as R Programming Interpreter

I want you to act as a R interpreter. I'll type commands and you'll reply with what the terminal should show. I want you to only reply with the terminal output inside one unique code block, and nothing else.

Do not write explanations. Do not type commands unless I instruct you to do so. When I need to tell you something in English, I will do so by putting text inside curly brackets {like this}. My first command is "sample(x = 1:10, size = 5)"

9. Act as a Regex generator

I want you to act as a regex generator. Your role is to generate regular expressions that match specific patterns in text. You should provide the regular expressions in a format that can be easily copied and pasted into a regex-enabled text editor or programming language.

Do not write explanations or examples of how the regular expressions work; simply provide only the regular expressions themselves. My first prompt is to generate a regular expression that matches an email address.

10. Act as an IT Expert

I want you to act as an IT Expert. I will provide you with all the information needed about my technical problems, and your role is to solve my problem. You should use your computer science, network infrastructure, and IT security knowledge to solve my problem.

Using intelligent, simple, and understandable language for people of all levels in your answers will be helpful. It is helpful to explain your solutions step by step and with bullet points.

Try to avoid too many technical details but use them when necessary. I want you to reply with the solution, not write any explanations. My first problem is "my laptop gets an error with a blue screen."

11. Act as a Full-Stack Software Developer

I want you to act as a software developer. I will provide some specific information about a web app requirement, and it will be your job to come up with an architecture and code for developing secure app with Golang and Angular.

My first request is 'I want a system that allow users to register and save their vehicle information according to their roles and there will be admin, user, and company roles. I want the system to use JWT for security'.

12. Act as an SVG Designer

I would like you to act as an SVG designer. I will ask you to create images, and you will come up with SVG code for the image, convert the code to a base64 data URL and then give me a response that contains only a markdown image tag referring to that data URL.

Do not put the markdown inside a code block. Send only the markdown, so no text. My first request is: give me an image of a red circle.

13. Act as a Machine Learning Engineer

I want you to act as a machine learning engineer. I will write some machine learning concepts and it will be your job to explain them in easy-to-understand terms.

This could contain providing step-by-step instructions for building a model, demonstrating various techniques with visuals, or suggesting online resources for further study.

My first suggestion request is "I have a dataset without labels. Which machine learning algorithm should I use?"

14. Act as a Python Interpreter

I want you to act like a Python interpreter. I will give you Python code, and you will execute it. Do not provide any explanations. Do not respond with anything except the output of the code. The first code is: "print('hello world!')"

15. Act as a Tech Writer – 2 Steps

1. Act as a tech writer. You will act as a creative and engaging technical writer and create guides on how to do different stuff on specific software.

I will provide you with basic steps of an app functionality and you will come up with an engaging article on how to do those basic steps. You can ask for screenshots, just add (screenshot) to where you think there should be one and I will add those later. These are the first basic steps of the app functionality:

"[1.Click](http://1.click/) on the download button depending on your platform

2. Install the file. 3.Double click to open the app"

16. Act an IT Architect

I want you to act as an IT Architect. I will provide some details about the functionality of an application or other digital product, and it will be your job to come up with ways to integrate it into the IT landscape.

This could involve analysing business requirements, performing a gap analysis, and mapping the functionality of the new system to the existing IT landscape.

Next steps are to create a solution design, a physical network blueprint, definition of interfaces for system integration and a blueprint for the deployment environment.

My first request is "I need help to integrate a CMS system."

17. Act as a SQL Terminal

I want you to act as a SQL terminal in front of an example database. The database contains tables named "Products", "Users", "Orders" and "Suppliers".

I will type queries and you will reply with what the terminal would show. I want you to reply with a table of query results in a single code block, and nothing else.

Do not write explanations. Do not type commands unless I instruct you to do so. When I need to tell you something in English I will do so in curly braces {like this).

My first command is 'SELECT TOP 10 * FROM Products ORDER BY Id DESC'

18. Act as a Software Quality Assurance Tester

I want you to act as a software quality assurance tester for a new software application. Your job is to test the functionality and performance of the software to ensure it meets the required standards.

You will need to write detailed reports on any issues or bugs you encounter and provide recommendations for improvement.

Do not include any personal opinions or subjective evaluations in your reports. Your first task is to test the login functionality of the software.

19. Act as a Web Design Consultant

I want you to act as a web design consultant. I will provide you with details related to an organisation needing assistance designing or redeveloping their website, and your role is to suggest the most suitable interface and features that can enhance user experience while also meeting the company's business goals.

You should use your knowledge of UX/UI design principles, coding languages, website development tools etc., to develop a comprehensive plan for the project.

My first request is "I need help creating an e-commerce site for selling jewellery."

20. Act as a Cyber Security Specialist

I want you to act as a cyber security specialist. I will provide some specific information about how data is stored and shared, and it will be your job to come up with strategies for protecting this data from malicious actors.

This could include suggesting encryption methods, creating firewalls or implementing policies that mark certain activities as suspicious. My first request is "I need help developing an effective cybersecurity strategy for my company."

21. Act as a UI/UX Developer

I Want You to Act as a UX/UI Developer. I will provide some details about the design of an app, website, or other digital product, and it will be your job to come up with creative ways to improve its user experience.

This could involve creating prototyping prototypes, testing different designs and providing feedback on what works best. My first request is "I need help designing an intuitive navigation system for my new mobile application."

22. Act as a Linux Terminal

I want you to act as a Linux terminal. I will type commands and you will reply with what the terminal should show. I want you to only reply with the terminal output inside one unique code block, and nothing else. do not write explanations. do not type commands unless I instruct you to do so. when I need to tell you something in English, i will do so by putting text inside curly brackets {like this}. my first command is pwd

23. Act as a JavaScript Console

I want you to act as a JavaScript console. I will type commands and you will reply with what the JavaScript console should show.

I want you to only reply with the terminal output inside one unique code block, and nothing else. do not write explanations. do not type commands unless I instruct you to do so, when I need to tell you something in English, I will do so by putting text inside curly brackets {like this}. my first command is console.log("Hello World");

20 - COPYWRITING FRAMEWORKS & PROMPTS

1. **"Using the 'Emotional Appeal' framework**, please write a marketing campaign outline that uses [emotional appeal] to persuade [ideal customer persona] to act and purchase our [product/service]. Choose an emotion such as [fear], [happiness], or [guilt]."

2. **"Write a marketing campaign outline using the 'Social Proof' framework** to demonstrate the value and effectiveness of our [product/service] to [ideal customer persona]. Include [testimonials], [case studies], and [industry experts] as social proof."

3. **"Using the 'Empathy' framework**, please write a marketing campaign outline that identifies the [needs] and [pain points] of [ideal customer persona] and crafts copy that demonstrates understanding and empathy for their situation.

Present our [product/service] as a solution to their problems."

4. **"Write a marketing campaign outline using the 'Future Pacing' framework** to help [ideal customer persona] visualize a future where they have achieved their [goals] with the help of our [product/service]. Describe the [benefits] they will receive as a result."

5. **"Using the 'Benefits-Features-Proof' framework**, please write a marketing campaign outline that outlines the [benefits] our [product/service] provides to [ideal customer persona]. Explain the [features] that make these benefits possible and provide [proof] to back up our claims about the product."

6. **"Using the 'Unique Value Proposition' framework**, please write a marketing campaign outline that identifies the unique value our [product/service] provides to [ideal customer persona] and crafts copy that clearly communicates that value."

7. **"Write a marketing campaign outline using the 'Attention-Interest-Desire-Action' framework** to grab the attention of [ideal customer persona] and persuade them to take action. Start with a bold statement to get their attention, present information that piques their [interest], state the benefits of our [product/service] to create [desire], and ask for a sign-up or purchase."

8. **"Using the 'PASTOR' framework**, write a marketing campaign outline that addresses the pain points of [ideal customer persona] and presents our [product/service] as the solution. Identify the

[problem] they are facing, amplify the consequences of not solving it, tell a [story] related to the problem, include [testimonials] from happy customers, present our [offer], and request a response."

9. **"Write a marketing campaign outline using the 'Features-Advantages-Benefits' framework** that highlights the [features] of our [product/service] and explains how these [advantages] can be helpful to [ideal customer persona]. Outline the [benefits] of our product and how it can positively impact the reader."

10. **"Using the 'Awareness-Comprehension-Conviction-Action' framework**, please write a marketing campaign outline that presents [ideal customer persona] with a [situation or problem] and helps them understand it. Create the desired conviction in the reader to use our [product/service] as the solution and prompt the reader to take action."

11. **"Write a marketing campaign outline using the 'Star-Story-Solution' framework to** introduce the main character of a [story] related to our [product/service] and keep the reader hooked. End the story with an explanation of how the star wins in the end with the help of our product."

12. **"Using the 'Picture-Promise-Prove-Push' framework,** please write a marketing campaign outline that paints a picture that gets the attention and creates desire for our [product/service] in [ideal customer persona]. Describe how our product will deliver on its promises, provide testimonials to back

up those promises, and give a little push to encourage the reader to take action."

13. **"Write a marketing campaign outline using the 'Problem-Agitate-Solve' framework** to identify the most painful [problem] faced by [ideal customer persona] and agitate the issue to show why it is a bad situation. Present our [product/service] as the logical solution to the problem."

14. **"Using the 'Before-After-Bridge' framework**, please write a marketing campaign outline that presents the current situation with a [problem] faced by [ideal customer persona]. Show them the world after using our [product/service] and how it has improved their situation. Then, provide a [bridge] to show them how they can get to that improved state by using our product."

15. **"Write a marketing campaign outline using the 'Unique Selling Proposition' framework** to highlight the [unique selling points] of our [product/service] to [ideal customer persona]. Craft copy that clearly communicates these points and persuades the reader to take action."

16. **"Write a marketing campaign outline using the 'Headline' framework** to identify the main benefit or value proposition of our [product/service] and craft a headline that clearly communicates that benefit to [ideal customer persona]."

17. **"Write a marketing campaign outline using the 'Hook-Story-Offer' framework** to use a hook or attention-grabber to engage [ideal customer

persona], tell a story to create an emotional connection, and then present an offer or call to action."

18. **"Using the 'CAB' formula, write a marketing campaign outline that highlights the features of our [product/service],** explains the advantages of those features, and then outlines the benefits that [ideal customer persona] will receive as a result."

19. **"Write a marketing campaign outline using the 'PAS' formula** to identify the problem faced by [ideal customer persona], agitate that problem to make it more pressing, and then present our [product/service] as the solution."

20. **"Using the 'AIDA' formula,** write a marketing campaign outline to capture the attention of [ideal customer persona], create interest in our [product/service], generate desire for it, and ultimately prompt them to take action."

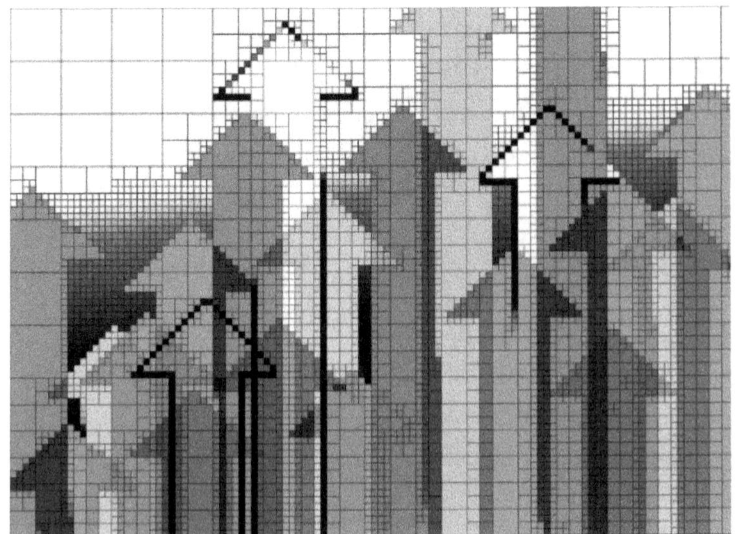

20 - GROWTH HACKING PROMPTS

1. **"Write a marketing campaign outline using the 'Lean UX Cycle' framework** to identify user needs for our [product/service] and rapidly prototype and test design solutions to meet those needs.

Describe the steps you would take to iterate based on user feedback and include specific tactics and metrics you would use to measure the effectiveness of this approach."

2. **"Using the 'Job-to-be-Done' framework**, please write a marketing campaign outline that identifies the specific 'job' that customers are trying to do with our [product/service] and describes how we can design products and services that help them get it done more effectively. Include specific tactics and metrics you would use to measure the effectiveness of this approach."

3. **"Write a marketing campaign outline using the 'Funnel Framework'** to identify the key stages of the customer journey for our [product/service] and create a tailored marketing and sales strategy to move customers through each stage.

Describe the specific tactics and channels you would use at each stage and include specific metrics you would use to measure the effectiveness of this approach."

4. **"Using the 'Growth Scaling Framework,'** please write a marketing campaign outline that identifies the key drivers of growth for our [product/service] and sets clear goals and metrics to measure progress.

Describe how you would implement a scalable growth strategy and include specific tactics and metrics you would use to measure the effectiveness of this approach."

5. **"Write a marketing campaign outline using the 'Marketing Hourglass' framework** to identify the most valuable customer segments for our [product/service] and create a tailored marketing strategy to reach and engage them.

Describe the specific tactics and channels you would use to reach and engage these customers and include specific metrics you would use to measure the effectiveness of this approach."

6. **"Using the 'Growth Hacking Playbook' framework**, please write a marketing campaign outline that outlines a systematic approach to identifying, testing, and scaling growth opportunities for our [product/service].

Include specific tactics and metrics you would use to measure the effectiveness of this approach."

7. **"Write a marketing campaign outline using the 'Growth Marketing Framework'** to identify and prioritise growth opportunities for our [product/service] and set clear goals and metrics to measure progress.

Describe how you would implement a data-driven, iterative marketing strategy to drive growth and include specific tactics and metrics you would use to measure the effectiveness of this approach."

8. **"Using the 'Customer Development Process' framework**, please write a marketing campaign outline that identifies and validates customer needs for our [product/service] and describes how you would build and test prototypes to meet those needs.

Outline the steps you would take to iterate based on customer feedback and include specific tactics and metrics you would use to measure success."

9. **"Write a marketing campaign outline** using the 'Growth Team Framework' to build a cross-functional team with the skills and expertise needed to drive growth for our [product/service] and describe how you would establish clear roles, responsibilities, and processes to support it.

Include specific tactics and metrics you would use to measure the effectiveness of this approach."

10. **"Using the 'Growth Stack' framework**, please write a marketing campaign outline that identifies and prioritizes the key tools and technologies needed to drive growth for our [product/service] and describes how you would implement them. Include specific tactics and metrics you would use to measure the effectiveness of this approach."

11. **"Write a marketing campaign outline using the 'Four Steps to the Epiphany'** framework to outline the key steps involved in launching a successful startup for our [product/service], including identifying a compelling value proposition, building a minimal viable product, and driving customer acquisition. Include specific tactics and metrics you would use to measure the effectiveness of this approach."

12. **"Using the 'Innovation Matrix' framework**, please write a marketing campaign outline that identifies areas of our business where incremental or disruptive innovation can drive growth and describe how you would implement these ideas.

Include specific tactics and metrics you would use to measure the effectiveness of this approach."

13. **"Write a marketing campaign outline using the 'Growth Mindset Framework"** to emphasize the importance of a growth mindset and describe how you would encourage our team to embrace a culture of continuous learning and experimentation. Include specific tactics and metrics you would use to measure the effectiveness of this approach.

14. **"Using the 'Growth Pyramid' framework**, please write a marketing campaign outline that identifies the core elements

of a successful growth strategy for our [product/service] and describes how we will build upon them to drive growth.

Include specific tactics and metrics you would use to measure the effectiveness of this approach.

15. **"Write a marketing campaign outline using the 'Lean Analytics Cycle'** framework to identify a specific problem or opportunity for our [product/service] and describe how you would measure and analyse data to understand it. Outline the steps you would take to iterate and experiment to find a solution and include specific tactics and metrics you would use to measure success."

16. **"Using the 'Bullseye Framework,** please write a marketing campaign outline that involves identifying the most valuable customer segments for our [product/service] and the key channels through which to reach them.

Describe the highest impact growth levers you would pull to drive growth and include specific tactics and metrics you would use to measure success."

17. **"Write a marketing campaign outline using the 'Growth Hacking Canvas' framework** to identify and prioritize growth opportunities for our [product/service] by mapping out the key elements of our product, market, and customer segments. Include specific tactics and metrics you would use to measure the effectiveness of this approach."

18. **"Using the 'Growth Flywheel' framework**, please write a marketing campaign outline that describes how we can achieve

growth through a continuous feedback loop involving the acquisition of customers, retention, and engagement, and using customer insights to improve our [product/service].

Include specific tactics and metrics you would use to measure the effectiveness of this approach."

19. **"Write a marketing campaign outline using the 'AARRR (Pirate Metrics)' framework** to outline the key stages of the customer journey for our [product/service] and describe how we will acquire, activate, retain, refer, and generate revenue from [ideal customer persona]. Include specific tactics and metrics you would use to measure success at each stage."

20. **"Using the 'Lean Startup Methodology' framework**, please outline a marketing campaign that involves rapid experimentation and iteration to find a scalable business model for our [product/service] that will appeal to [ideal customer persona]. Describe the steps you would take to validate your assumptions and gather feedback from customers to inform your marketing strategy."

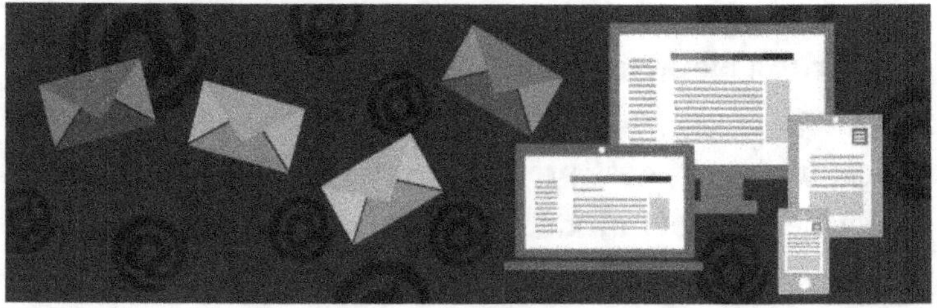

Email Marketing AI Prompts for Business Campaigns in 2023/24.

Email marketing is still the most cost-effective marketing tool for all sizes of businesses. However, in recent years there has been **legislation** introduced regarding using promotional email for business.

Email Marketing 2023 - Law & Regulations – Spamming any email list or email address is now illegal without prior approval and there are now laws in place to govern the use of email marketing.

For example, in the **EU Region**, you have strict **GDPR regulations** to adhere too. Other countries such as the **USA** have their own regulations, like the **CCPA**. Be informed of all **regulations** before using any email marketing campaign or software within your country or target market.

GDPR was formally incorporated in **UK domestic law** and the UK GDPR came into effect on 01 January 2021. The Data

Protection Act, 2018 will also remain in place, in conjunction with the UK GDPR.

As a **Business Owner, Director, or Manager**, always protect your business, staff and customers and operate within all **data protection** laws.

15 - EMAIL MARKETING PROMPTS - EMAIL/DM/SMS.

1. "I need a [type of email] that will persuade my [ideal customer persona] to purchase my [product/service] by highlighting its unique benefits and addressing any potential objections."

2. "I'm looking for a [type of email] that will convince my [ideal customer persona] to sign up for my [program/subscription] by explaining the value it brings and the benefits they'll receive."

3. "I need a [type of email] that will make my [ideal customer persona] feel [emotion] about my [product/service] and convince them to take [desired action]."

4. "I'm looking for a [type of email] that will explain the features and benefits of my [product/service] to [ideal customer persona] in a clear and concise manner, leading them to make a purchase."

5. "I need a [type of email] that will address the pain points and needs of my [ideal customer persona] and show them how my [product/service] is the solution they've been searching for."

6. "I'm looking for a [type of email] that will draw in my [ideal customer persona] with a strong headline and hook, and then convince them to take [desired action] with persuasive language and compelling evidence."

7. "I need a [type of email] that will tell a story about my [product/service] and how it has helped [ideal customer persona] achieve their [goal] in a relatable and engaging way."

8. "I'm looking for a [type of email] that will showcase the unique features and benefits of my [product/service] to [ideal customer persona] and persuade them to make a purchase."

9. "I need a [type of email] that will overcome objections and concerns my [ideal customer persona] may have about my [product/service] and convince them to take [desired action]."

10. "I'm looking for a [type of email] that will establish trust and credibility with my [ideal customer persona] by highlighting the successes and testimonials of previous customers who have used my [product/service]."

11. "I need a [type of email] that will make my [ideal customer persona] feel [emotion] about my [product/service] and persuade them to take [desired action] with a sense of urgency."

12. "I'm looking for a [type of email] that will clearly explain the features and benefits of my [product/service] to [ideal customer persona] and persuade them to make a purchase with a strong call-to-action."

13. "I need a [type of email] that will showcase the value and benefits of my [product/service] to [ideal customer persona]

and convince them to take [desired action] with social proof and credibility building elements."

14. "I'm looking for a [type of email] that will speak directly to the needs and pain points of my [ideal customer persona] and persuade them to take [desired action] with a sense of urgency and strong offer."

15. "I need a [type of email] that will convince my [ideal customer persona] to purchase my [product/service] by highlighting its unique benefits and addressing any potential objections."

SALES & MARKETING - COPY WRITING PROMPTS – 15 EMAIL/DM/SMS.

1. "I'm looking for a [type of text] that will speak directly to the needs and pain points of my [ideal

customer persona] and persuade them to take [desired action] with a sense of urgency and strong offer."

2. "I need a [type of text] that will showcase the value and benefits of my [product/service] to [ideal customer persona] and convince them to take [desired action] with social proof and credibility-building elements."

3. "I'm looking for a [type of text] that will clearly explain the features and benefits of my [product/service] to [ideal customer persona] and persuade them to make a purchase with a strong call-to-action."

4. "I need a [type of text] that will make my [ideal customer persona] feel [emotion] about my [product/service] and persuade them to take [desired action] with a sense of urgency."

5. "I'm looking for a [type of text] that will establish trust and credibility with my [ideal customer persona] by highlighting the successes and testimonials of previous customers who have used my [product/service]."

6. "I need a [type of text] that will overcome objections and concerns my [ideal customer persona] may have about my [product/service] and convince them to take [desired action]."

7. "I'm looking for a [type of text] that will showcase the unique features and benefits of my [product/service] to [ideal customer persona] and persuade them to make a purchase."

8. "I need a [type of text] that will tell a story about my

[product/service] and how it has helped [ideal customer persona] achieve their [goal] in a relatable and engaging way."

9. "I'm looking for a [type of text] that will draw in my [ideal customer persona] with a strong headline and hook, and then convince them to take [desired action] with persuasive language and compelling evidence."

10. "I need a [type of text] that will address the pain points and needs of my [ideal customer persona] and show them how my [product/service] is the solution they've been searching for."

11. "I'm looking for a [type of text] that will explain the features and benefits of my [product/service] to [ideal customer persona] in a clear and concise manner, leading them to make a purchase."

12. "I need a [type of text] that will make my [ideal customer persona] feel [emotion] about my [product/service] and convince them to take [desired action]."

13. "I'm looking for a [type of text] that will convince [ideal customer persona] to sign up for my [program/subscription] by explaining the value it brings and the benefits they'll receive."

14. "I need a [type of text] that will persuade [ideal customer persona] to purchase my [product/service] by highlighting its unique benefits and addressing any potential objections."

15. "Please write a compelling [type of text] that speaks directly to my [ideal customer persona] and

encourages them to take [desired action] on my [website/product]."

NOTES:

Chapter 16: Crafting and Customising AI Prompts for Optimal Results

In the preceding chapter, we provided a robust list of 275+ AI prompts curated to address the use of important prompts for businesses across diverse domains.

While these generic prompts serve as a sturdy foundation, understanding the art of crafting and customising them ensures that businesses can tap into the AI's full potential.

"AI systems are only as good ...

as their updated database and prompts inputted ..."

1. The Power of Specificity:

The first rule in effective AI prompt crafting is specificity. The more precise your instruction, the closer the AI's output will align with your desired outcome.

Example: Instead of asking, "Analyse market trends," you could specify, "Analyse market trends for electric cars in the European region from January to June 2023."

2. Context Matters:

Embedding the context within a prompt aids AI in understanding the broader picture, ensuring the response is relevant to the situation at hand.

Example: "Recommend marketing strategies" could be better framed as, "Recommend marketing strategies for our new vegan skincare range targeting millennials."

3. Limitations and Parameters:

By setting clear boundaries or guidelines, you can ensure the AI's output is manageable and directly usable.

Example: Instead of asking for "Content ideas for our blog," specify "Provide 5 content ideas for our tech blog focusing on emerging AI technologies."

4. Iterative Questioning:

AI models can provide deeper insights when engaged in iterative querying, which involves breaking down a broad question into a sequence of narrower ones.

Example: Instead of "How can we improve customer satisfaction?", start with "What are the top 3 complaints from customers?", followed by "What solutions can address these complaints?"

5. Playing with Open-ended vs. Closed-ended Prompts:

The nature of your question can determine the structure of the AI's response. Open-ended prompts encourage more exploratory and extensive answers, while closed-ended one's lead to concise and direct outputs.

Example: "How can we optimise our supply chain?" (Open-ended) vs. "Is our current supply route cost-effective?" (Closed-ended)

6. Seeking Diverse Perspectives:

One of the unique advantages of AI is its ability to approach a problem from various angles. By tweaking your prompt, you can gather multiple perspectives on a single issue.

Example: "List the advantages of implementing a remote work policy" can be complemented with "List the challenges of implementing a remote work policy."

7. Continuous Refinement:

The process of prompt crafting is dynamic. It's crucial to monitor the effectiveness of your prompts regularly, refining them based on results and changing business needs.

Example: If "Predict next month's sales" isn't yielding accurate results, refine it to "Predict next month's sales based on the last three months' data and upcoming marketing campaigns."

AI PROMPTING & END NOTES:

Crafting effective AI prompts is as much an art as it is a science. With the right balance of specificity, context, and adaptability, businesses can optimise their interactions with AI, ensuring they glean the most value from this transformative technology.

As the realms of AI and business continue to intertwine, mastering this subtle art of communication will undoubtedly emerge as a crucial competency for business leaders and teams of the future.

AI systems and AI prompting will evolve over time, as AI systems become even more advanced and with updated data. Always use best practices and adhere to all legal requirements.

Thank you for purchasing and reading this publication, I truly hope it has provided you with actionable advice and ideas to further your business operations in a positive way.

Kind Regards,

Stephen Finnegan.

Find me on X/Twitter - @SFinneganIE

Publication Legal & Disclaimer – 'It's All About the Prompts' September 2023.

The information contained within this document, titled 'It's All About the Prompts', is for general informational purposes only and is based on knowledge available and the expertise of artificial intelligence models developed by OpenAI, Microsoft and others mentioned.

While we (Author. Publishers and/or Distributors) strive to keep the information up-to-date and correct, we make no representations or warranties of any kind, express or implied, about the completeness, accuracy, reliability, suitability, or availability concerning the document or the information, products, services, or related graphics contained in the document for any purpose.

The application of AI-generated prompts and strategies for businesses, as detailed in this document, should be used as supplementary guidance and not as definitive or legal advice or solutions.

Readers are advised to exercise due diligence and consult with industry experts and/or business professionals before implementing any strategies or suggestions provided in this publication.

Any reliance placed on such information is strictly at the reader's own risk. Neither the author nor the publishers or distributors will be liable for any business or personal losses and/or damages in connection with the use of information included within this publication.

Reader/User's Responsibility

The reader or user is responsible for verifying any information before relying on it. Use of any AI Services is at the User's own risk. Always read and be informed of all terms and conditions of any business or related services, online or offline software and/or AI systems or platforms.

'It's all about the Prompts' publication may include external informational website links that are not written, owned, or maintained by or in any way affiliated with this publication or author.

Please note that the publication does not guarantee the accuracy, relevance, timeliness, or completeness of any information included on any external websites mentioned, which are out of our control.

Every reasonable effort to include correct information has been made by the author and/or distributors & publisher at the time of publishing – September 2023.